LifeWay Kids & FOR GIRLS
PRESENT

God's Brave Girl

A COURAGEOUS JOURNEY OF FAITH

LEADER GUIDE
LIFEWAY PRESS®
NASHVILLE, TN

Requests for permission should
be addressed in writing to
LifeWay Press®
One LifeWay Plaza
Nashville, TN 37234-0172

ISBN 978-1-535999-07-6
Item 005823164

Dewey Decimal Classification Number:
268.432
Subject Heading: Discipleship—Cur-
ricula\God\Bible—Study
Dewey Decimal Classification Number:
248.82
Subject Heading: CHRISTIAN LIFE \
JESUS CHRIST—TEACHINGS

Printed in the United States
of America
LifeWay Kids
LifeWay Resources
One LifeWay Plaza
Nashville, Tennessee 37234-0172

Cover design: Julia Ryan

We believe the Bible has God for its
author; salvation for its end; and truth,
without any mixture of error, for its
matter and that all Scripture is totally
true and trustworthy. To review Life-
Way's doctrinal guideline, please visit
lifeway.com/doctrinalguideline.

All Scripture quotations are taken from
the Christian Standard Bible®, Copyright
2017 by Holman Bible Publishers. Used
by permission. Christian Standard Bible®
and CSB® are federally registered trade-
marks of Holman Bible Publishers.

About the Authors

Jonathan & Wynter Pitts:
FOUNDERS OF FOR GIRLS LIKE YOU

Wynter Pitts is the author of several books and the
founder of For Girls Like You, a bimonthly magazine
that equips girls to be who God has created them to
be and to resource their parents to raise strong, Christ-
following girls. Wynter tragically passed from death to
life on July 24, 2018, after 15 years of marriage to her
beloved Jonathan.

Jonathan Pitts is an author, speaker, and executive
pastor at Church of the City in Franklin, Tennessee,
where he lives with his four daughters. Prior to
pastoring, Jonathan was executive director at The
Urban Alternative, the national ministry of Dr. Tony
Evans in Dallas, Texas.

Danielle Bell:
A GIRL JUST LIKE YOU!

Danielle has over 24 years of children's ministry
experience and is a respected children's ministry leader
and trainer. She has spoken regionally and nationally at
children's ministry conferences (i.e., Children's Pastors
Conference, ETCH, KidMin conference). She has written
for The Gospel Project for Kids, and she currently works
with Outreach Media Group writing preschool and
elementary lessons for Sermons4Kids. She also teaches
as part of the children's ministry certification program
at beadisciple.com. Danielle's blog, dandibell.com, was
named one of the top 100 kids ministry blogs by
ministry-to-children.com.

Table of Contents

A Note from Jonathan Pitts

I am so glad you are holding this resource and leading girls to learn about who they are and who God calls them to be. My wife, Wynter, started *For Girls Like You* because we had four girls (Alena, Kaitlyn, Camryn, and Olivia) she wanted to influence—specifically our oldest, Alena, who was 7 at the time. Wynter had a desire for our daughters to experience the things they love without the negative messages and imagery that often appears in entertainment.

And so, the ministry was humbly launched out of our house on a borrowed laptop in 2012 with little more than a dream. Wynter combined her dreams with simple obedience and poured her heart and soul into creating the *For Girls Like You* magazine. In 2015, she published her first book, *For Girls Like You: A Devotional for Tweens*. Miraculously, she published seven more books in just three years.

And then our world changed when my family suffered an unspeakable loss. Wynter unexpectedly went home to be with the Lord on the evening of Tuesday, July 24, 2018, in Dallas, Texas. She was just 38 years old. In the days that followed, the ministry team and I took comfort in knowing two things. First, that Wynter finished her race. She ran it well, accomplished God's purposes for her life, and then she went home. Second, that Wynter left us with a job to do. I'll never forget the sense of purpose God gave me in making sure that Wynter's heart, vision, and legacy continue on.

We continue to publish the *For Girls Like You* magazine as well as provide additional resources for tween girls and their parents in honor of her memory and to help fulfill her mission and vision: to empower and equip girls to walk boldly into becoming who God has created them to be and to provide parents with the support needed to raise strong Christ followers.

Today, *For Girls Like You* continues to grow and thrive. I am amazed at what God is doing with Wynter's dream. I think Wynter would be delighted in knowing we continue to disciple young hearts—where this ministry first began.

I miss my wife. I am grateful for the 15 years of marriage we shared, and I see Wynter reflected in our four beautiful daughters every day. I am honored to keep her ministry impact and legacy alive through *For Girls Like You*, and I would invite you and the tween girls in your life to join us there as we seek to follow Jesus.

Sharing the Gospel with Girls

During these next six weeks we want you to be ready to share the gospel with your girls. Remember these key tips as you talk about the gospel and how girls can have a relationship with Jesus.

- ♡ The truths of the Bible are for your girls right now. The ultimate goal of teaching the Bible is for her to see who God made her to be and to trust in Jesus as her Savior. The Holy Spirit is the leader in the experience, but we have the responsibility of following the Spirit's leading.

- ♡ Becoming a Christian is an individual matter. Take the time to discuss what it means to trust in Jesus in a one-on-one conversation. When you make space to talk to each girl about what God is doing in her heart and life, she will feel more free to share true thoughts and feelings.

- ♡ Remember that each person comes to this important decision as the Holy Spirit leads. People come from all different backgrounds and respond at different ages. Strive to know the girls you teach as individuals.

- ♡ Use your Bible as you share the gospel. After reading a Bible verse, be ready to explain the verse in your own words. Invite the girls also to read in their own Bibles to see this truth for themselves. Help them understand unfamiliar terms such as *sin* and *repent*.

- ♡ Help the girls know how they can respond. Use questions that require thoughtful answers rather than just yes or no. Use language your girls understand such as: Tell God you know you have sinned and are sorry. Ask God to forgive you for your sin, for wanting your way instead of God's way. Ask Jesus to become your Savior and Lord.

- ♡ Include parents or caregivers when possible. Tell them what led you to discuss salvation with their child. Explain where you think their girl is in her spiritual journey (e.g., becoming aware of a need for God, is thoughtfully considering how to respond, made a decision to trust in Jesus, and so forth).

- ♡ Pray. Ask God's leadership as you help the girls grow in their understanding of salvation.

How to Use this Guide

LEADER GUIDE

For Girls Like You: God's Brave Girl Leader Guide (9781535999076) takes girls on a journey through six weeks of Bible study and discussion about how to live bravely in today's world. Girls are being told to be brave—to live confidently and make choices that are brave for their world. Yet young girls need to understand why they can live bravely in the context of who God is and who He created them to be. Living a brave life means living a life of faith and trust in God, boldly following where He leads. Girls can learn from the Bible what living bravely means and how God has uniquely gifted and equipped them for His plans for their lives.

This study brings vibrant, fun, and relevant experiences that girls are used to seeing in the *For Girls Like You* family of products. This leader guide can be used in church for any size group or in a family setting. This book provides detailed plans for each of the six sessions. *For Girls Like You: God's Brave Girl Digital Leader Guide* (9781535999717) is available for purchase at lifeway.com/godsbravegirl.

STUDY JOURNALS FOR GIRLS

Each girl will need a copy of her own *For Girls Like You: God's Brave Girl Study Journal* for her age range. These journals are designed to be used both during each session and individually during the week. Each journal provides fun activities that correspond with each session as well as weekly devotions to use at home. More information and resources are available for purchase at lifeway.com/godsbravegirl and forgirlslikeyou.com.

PRINTABLES

Included in this Leader Guide is a download code to download and print additional items used throughout each session. To access your free downloadable items, go to my.lifeway.com/redeem and register or log in.

Enter the following code to download your printable items:

F7PNWWI328

Study Journals

For Girls Like You: God's Brave Girl Study Journals are designed just for girls! On the first few pages of each session girls will find the Bible story and fun activities to complete with other girls in the group.

There are pages set apart for each girl to use on her own each week. These pages will help her spend time with God, pray, and learn more about herself.

Finally, there are some extra fun games, riddles, puzzles, and more!

The *Younger Girls Study Journal* (9781535999113) and *Older Girls Study Journal* (9781535999120) are available for purchase at lifeway.com/godsbravegirl and forgirlslikeyou.com.

Brave to BELIEVE GOD

Leader Bible Study

Being a girl is challenging. If you are raising girls or teaching girls, you know that the world is bombarding them with lies at an alarming rate. The world often defines a brave girl as someone who follows her heart, puts on a mask of someone else's expectations, or trusts in herself instead of God—and many girls are believing in these ideas.

The Bible gives a different definition of bravery. In Joshua 1:9 God tells the new leader of Israel, Joshua, what true bravery looks like. *"Haven't I commanded you: be strong and courageous? Do not be afraid or discouraged, for the LORD your God is with you wherever you go"* (emphasis added). The source of bravery comes not from ourselves but from God. Throughout this study, you will lead girls on a journey of what God's Word teaches about bravery. As you explore God's truth, your girls can recognize and live out true bravery because they have confidence in the One who calls them to live bravely.

In this session you will guide the girls to understand that bravery begins by believing God is who He says He is. Before you teach, consider taking a moment to reflect on the last time you encountered Jesus. Maybe it was through prayer, reading His Word, a conversation with a friend, or in worship with other believers.

Take a moment to be still before the Lord and reflect on who you know God to be. Remember how He has shown you that He is worthy of your trust.

Read and reflect on the following Bible verses as you consider these truths: Exodus 14:14; Joshua 1:9; Isaiah 40:31; Psalm 27:1; Mark 11:24; John 8:36; Romans 10:9-10; Philippians 4:6-7. As the Holy Spirit brings truths to your mind, take a moment to write them down.

Pray aloud the things you have written that describe who you know God to be. Remember these truths as you embark on this journey of pointing girls to Jesus so they will know Him and live as the brave girls God made them to be!

KEY TRUTH:
Jesus came to make our relationship with God possible. He calls us to believe He is who He says He is.

KEY VERSE:
I have come so that they may have life and have it in abundance. John 10:10

KEY PASSAGE:
Mary Saw Jesus (John 20:1-18)

Get Started!

SAY THE NAME

YOU WILL NEED:
☐ A blanket or bedsheet thick enough not to see through

TEACHING TIP: Invite the girls to introduce themselves before playing the game.

Form two groups and instruct each group to stand on either side of the blanket. Invite two leaders to hold up the blanket. Give each group around ten seconds to pick which girl will stand facing the blanket opposite the other team. Once both teams have their player chosen, the leaders will count to three and drop the blanket.

Each player will try to say the name of the girl standing across from her before the other player does. The player who says the correct name first earns a point for her team. If she says the incorrect name, the other player gets a chance to say the name of the girl across from her. Play continues until each girl has had a turn or as time permits.

Invite the girls to sit in a circle and discuss the game using the following question prompts.

♡ What was hard about the game?

♡ What made the game easy to play?

♡ How did you feel right before the leaders lowered the blanket for you to see who was on the other side?

♡ If you were to play again, how would you make the game more challenging?

Say: To be successful in this game, you had to know the other person's name to call it first. The better you knew the other player, the easier it was to identify her quickly and call her name. Today, we are going to learn about someone from the Bible who had a close relationship with Jesus. We'll see how knowing Jesus encouraged her to be brave during a tough time.

Bible Story

YOU WILL NEED:
- ☐ Strips of construction paper
- ☐ Markers
- ☐ Masking tape

masking tape ▬

TO DO:
- ☐ Make an outline of a cross shape on the floor with masking tape. (See example.)

Give each girl a strip of paper and a marker.

Say: Fear is real, isn't it? We all have dealt with fear before, maybe even this week. Hold the paper strip in your hand. Think about something that might make you or someone you know fearful. When you have thought of something, either write down that fear or draw a picture to represent it on your strip of paper.

Give the girls time to complete this activity and then invite them to lay their strips of paper on the outline of the cross on the floor. Remind the girls that they can lay their strips of paper facedown if they don't want others to see what they wrote. Once everyone has her strip of paper inside the cross, continue.

Say: Today, we are going to learn about what the Bible says about God, about us, and about bravery. We're going to learn about who God is, why we can trust Him, and how He wants us to live our lives. Today's true story from the Bible is about a friend of Jesus who was sad and afraid after Jesus died on the cross. Even though she was sad, she showed great bravery to believe God even when other people doubted.

Continue: After Jesus died, His friends took Him down from the cross, wrapped His body in strips of cloth, and put His body in a tomb. A large rock was placed in front of the tomb. His friends were very sad. Mary Magdalene, the person we are learning about today from the Bible, was one of Jesus' friends. She cared about Jesus very much. She knew that He loved her even though she wasn't perfect, and she was heartbroken when He died. Today's true story picks up when Mary goes to visit Jesus' tomb. Let's see how this story teaches us about how Mary was brave to believe God.

Mary Saw Jesus
(JOHN 20:1-18)

On the third day after Jesus' death, Mary Magdalene (MAG duh leen) went out to Jesus' tomb. It was still dark, and she saw that the large stone at the entrance had been moved away.

Mary ran to tell Peter and John, two of Jesus' friends, what she had seen. "They have taken the Lord out of the tomb, and we don't know where they have put Him!" she said.

Peter and John ran to the tomb. John looked inside and saw the linen cloths they had used to wrap Jesus' body lying inside. Then Peter went into the tomb and saw the linen cloths too. The cloth that had been around Jesus' head was folded up. John believed that Jesus was alive. Then Peter and John went back home.

Mary stood outside the tomb and cried. When she looked inside, she saw two angels sitting there. They said to her, "Woman, why are you crying?"

"Because they've taken away my Lord, and I don't know where they've put Him," she responded. Then Mary turned around. Jesus stood in front of her, but she did not recognize Him.

Jesus said, "Woman, why are you crying? Who are you looking for?"

Mary thought Jesus might be the gardener. She replied, "Sir, if you have taken Jesus away, tell me where you've put Him and I will go get Him."

Jesus said, "Mary."

Mary turned around and said, "Teacher!" Jesus sent Mary to tell the other disciples that He was going back to the Father. Mary did what Jesus said and told the disciples, "I have seen the Lord!"

Make The Point

Say: When Mary arrived at the tomb, the stone had been removed and only the strips of cloths that had been wrapped around Jesus' body remained. That must have been so scary! Jesus was gone and Mary didn't understand what happened. But once Jesus revealed Himself to her, she knew that she had seen the Lord, and her fear vanished.

Explain: Mary wasn't brave because she had gotten over her fear. She was brave because she looked to Jesus and believed in Him. **Jesus calls us to believe He is who He says He is.** This is where true bravery begins. We can be brave because we know that God is God and He is trustworthy. We can trust that He is always with us, even when we are afraid. Being brave doesn't mean scary things won't still happen or our fears go away and never return. Being God's brave girl means trusting that God is in control and putting our confidence and trust in Him, even when we are afraid, uncertain, or walking through difficult times.

Bible Study

I Have Seen the Lord

YOU WILL NEED:
- ☐ Study Journals (1 per girl)
- ☐ Pens (1 per girl)

TO DO:
- ☐ Distribute a study journal to each girl and give her a pen or pencil.

Distribute a study journal to each girl. Explain to the group that each session there will be fun activities in their books to complete to help them learn more about God and their relationship with Him. Point out the daily devotional and journal pages that the girls can use throughout this study. Explain that after each session, the girls may take their books home to continue growing in their relationship with God.

Invite the girls to open their study journals to "I Have Seen the Lord" (pg. 8). Explain that you or a volunteer will read each section aloud. Encourage the girls to listen carefully as the passage is read, possibly even closing their eyes to focus. Then invite them to open their eyes and draw what they think Mary's expression could have been based on that section of the story.

Read the following Bible passages or invite a volunteer to read these passages aloud: John 20:1-2; John 20:3-11; John 20:12-13; John 20:14-15; John 20:16-18.

Remind the girls that even though they don't know for sure what emotions were on Mary's face, they can use their imaginations to consider what her expressions might have been. After they have drawn an expression for each Bible passage, discuss what they drew and why.

Ask: Were there any sections that were easy to imagine how Mary's face might have looked? Were there any parts that were difficult? *(Allow for answers.)*

Say: Imagine if you were Mary in that situation—a faithful friend of Jesus who was grieving His death and didn't really understand everything that was happening. Even as you cried and were sad, you made your way to His tomb, only to realize that He wasn't there. What thoughts would have gone through your head? What do you think your reaction might have been? *(Allow responses.)*

Continue: Now imagine later that you heard Jesus' voice call your name. What would your reaction be when you looked and realized it really was Jesus calling your name? *(Allow for discussion.)*

Say: Mary Magdalene knew Jesus as Savior, Lord, teacher, and friend. She believed Jesus was who He said He was—the Promised Messiah. Mary was not brave on her own. Her bravery was based on who she knew Jesus to be! **Jesus also calls us to believe that He is who He says He is.** True bravery comes from confidence in who God is and who He calls us to be.

JESUS IS WORTH SEEING

YOU WILL NEED:
- [ ] Study Journals (1 per girl)
- [ ] Pens or pencils (1 per girl)
- [ ] Bibles (1 per girl)

TO DO:
- [ ] Consider marking the pages in the Bible where the passages can be found.

TEACHING TIP: Be aware of girls who are not familiar with a Bible. Show them where to look for each book on the contents page or hand them Bibles where you have already marked the verses. This might be a great activity for the girls to do in pairs to get to know one another better as they open God's Word.

Invite each girl to open her study journal to "Jesus Is Worth Seeing" (pg. 9). Guide the girls to work in small groups of two or three to look up each verse or passage and fill in the blank that helps describe who Jesus is. Once they have completed the activity, discuss which description of Jesus stuck out to them.

Ask: As you learned about Jesus:

♡ What verse meant the most to you?

♡ Why do you think it meant the most to you?

♡ Which verse was easy to believe about Jesus? Why?

♡ Which verse was difficult to believe about Jesus? Why?

If time allows, invite the girls to complete "Key Code" in their study journals by solving the code to uncover today's key truth (pg. 8).

Say: Girls, you can believe that Jesus is who He says He is. He is more than we can imagine. When we look to Him, He can help us bravely follow Him. In this study we are going to pray together. Prayer is simply talking and listening to God. It isn't fancy or formal. God loves us and He wants us to talk with Him.

Pray: Invite the group to pray together, repeating each statement after you either aloud or silently from the following prayer:

Jesus thank you for being:

- ♡ *The Bread of Life*
- ♡ *The Light of the World*
- ♡ *The Door of the Sheep*
- ♡ *The Good Shepherd*

- ♡ *The Resurrection and the Life*
- ♡ *The Way, the Truth, and the Life*
- ♡ *The True Vine*

Give us eyes to see You, Jesus, and hearts to believe You are who You say You are. In You alone we can be brave and trust You! In Jesus' name, amen.

Small Group Activities

BELIEVE IT OR NOT

YOU WILL NEED:
- ☐ Item 4: Believe It or Not Signs
- ☐ Masking tape

TO DO:
- ☐ Print Item 4: Believe It or Not Signs.
- ☐ Hang the "BELIEVE IT" and "NOT TRUE" signs on opposite walls.
- ☐ Create a tape line down the middle of the room with masking tape, dividing the play area into two sides.

Say: Today's key verse comes from John 10:10. It says, "I have come so that they may have life and have it in abundance." Abundance means something beyond what is expected, imagined, or hoped for. This verse is saying that Jesus came so that we could have something better than we can ever imagine—a restored relationship with God, the One who made us and loves us. We learn about God's abundant love for us through His Word, the Bible, and that leads us to look to Him and trust Him no matter what. That is what God's brave girl looks like.

Sometimes we can get confused about what true bravery is. It can be easier to believe what people around us say about bravery because those ideas sound good or easy, but we always need to examine what is true by comparing what we hear to what the Bible tells us. Let's consider some of these ideas and decide if they match up to what God says.

Show the girls the "BELIEVE IT" and "NOT TRUE" signs on opposite walls. Explain that they will move to either side of the room depending on if they believe the statement they hear is true or not true. Read each of the following statements and give the girls time to choose their sides. Invite a few girls to share why they chose each side. Gently point out the truth with each statement.

01. The best way to be brave is to follow your heart. (NOT TRUE—We often want to listen to our hearts and our feelings, but our hearts can't always be trusted. In Jeremiah 17:9, we learn that the heart is deceitful. Instead of following our hearts, we should follow the true words that God gives us in the Bible.)

02. I can do all things through Christ who gives me strength. (BELIEVE IT— The Bible says, "I am able to do all things through him who strengthens me" (Phil. 4:13). God chose Paul, one of Jesus' followers, to write this verse in the Bible to remind us that we can trust God no matter what. Mary was brave because she put her trust in Jesus. She recognized and believed that she needed a Savior and that Jesus is who He says He is!)

03. God will not give you any more than you can handle on your own. (NOT TRUE—This world is a tough place and there will be times when things may be too hard for us to handle on our own. We may experience heartache, loss, pain, or injustice that we could never carry alone. Look at Mary; she was Jesus' friend, and she was absolutely heartbroken at His death. Girls, this is why we need Jesus. We don't have to cry alone, fight alone, grieve alone, or suffer alone. Psalm 34:18 says, "The LORD is close to the brokenhearted; he saves those crushed in spirit." No matter what you are going through, God promises to always be with you.)

04. I need God's help to be brave. (BELIEVE IT—Yes! Admitting this is not a sign of weakness. You don't have to pretend to have it all together. Mary was afraid and sad until she saw Jesus. Seeing and believing Jesus gave her the help and confidence she needed to be brave! See John 20:18.)

05. Being brave doesn't mean that I have to be perfect. (BELIEVE IT—Girls, give yourselves a break! We can't be perfect. God alone is perfect. Romans 8:1 tells us that we are forgiven when we trust in Jesus. God simply asks you to believe that He is who He says He is.)

Say: The world is throwing all kinds of ideas at you about what bravery is, but God wants you to compare every idea to His true Word. God is true and trustworthy and **He calls us to believe He is who He says He is.**

GUESS WHO

Invite the girls to play a round of charades where each girl will act out a person, object, or animal she chooses. The rest of the girls will take turns guessing who the actress is portraying. Play several rounds as time allows.

Say: That was fun! You girls did a great job of acting out different people, objects, and animals. Today, we are thinking more about how Jesus calls us to believe He is who He says He is. That means that we don't have to guess who Jesus is. The Bible teaches us who Jesus is and what He is like.

Ask: Who do you believe Jesus to be? *(Allow the girls to answer honestly and ask questions. Remember, you don't have to have all of the answers. Prayerfully trust the Holy Spirit to prompt your group for open and honest discussion. It is in finding Jesus that these girls will find the true source of bravery.)*

Explain: God loves each one of us so much that He sent His only Son, Jesus, to earth to rescue us. The Bible tells us that we have a big problem. We have disobeyed God and believed what we want to do is better than God's plan for us. Choosing your way and disobeying God is a big deal. We may not like to admit it, but we are not perfect. We make decisions we later regret and choose to do what we want to do instead of what God wants us to do. We deserve the consequences of our wrong choices, but God sent His Son Jesus to pay the price our sin deserves—death. **Jesus came to make our relationship with God possible.** He took all of our lies, all of our bad attitudes, all of our selfish thoughts and actions, and even all of our fears of not trusting God. When we trust in Jesus, we are called His daughters. (See Hebrews 2:10.)

Pray: Invite the group to pray together, repeating each statement after you either aloud or silently from the prayer below:

Jesus, help us see You for who You are.
When we see You, help us believe.
As we believe, help us look to You to be brave.

We need You, Jesus. Amen.

Conclusion

Give each girl a rock and a marker. Invite the girls to sit quietly in front of the "Names of Jesus" sign. Challenge them to read through the names, allowing a moment to reflect on each name. Then ask them to choose one name that stands out to them and to write that name on the provided rock. Allow the girls to share why they wrote that particular name on their rocks as they decorate them.

Say: Girls, we are going to have a time of personal prayer and reflection. Prayer doesn't have to be a formal event. Praying is simply talking and listening to God. Just be you as you silently talk to Him, and I will close us in prayer.

Guide the girls to find a quiet place in the room to hold their rocks as they pray. Consider playing soft worship music as they pray.

Say: As you sit quietly in your space, pray and ask God to show you more about Jesus. *(Allow a few minutes for the girls to reflect and pray.)* Pray that He would help you see Jesus as the name you wrote on your rock. *(Allow the girls to reflect and pray.)* Think about anything else that you want to talk to God about.

Pray: *God, if we are honest, sometimes we allow our feelings or situations to change our focus of how we think about You. Help us see You as You are and help us believe that You are who You say You are. In Jesus' name, amen.*

Finish: Girls, I hope you learned something new about God today. This week, keep exploring who Jesus is and who He made you to be by working through your study journal. Write down any questions or thoughts you may have. Jesus can help you be brave and trust Him this week.

SESSION TWO

Brave to TRUST GOD'S PLAN

Leader Bible Study

A future filled with unknowns and uncertainty often leads to doubts and worry. So often what we believe about God when difficult situations come reflects our level of trust in Him. If we don't see God as honest and perfect, we may have reservations about whether His plans are best. This is where we are often tempted to believe the lie that tells us we know better—and then teach it to our girls. But we must remember that His ways are not our ways and He is a God we can depend on yesterday, today, and tomorrow. (See Isaiah 55:8-9.) Spend some time alone with God and ask yourself these questions:

♡ Do I believe God is an honest, perfect God? Do my actions reflect what I believe? Why or why not?

KEY TRUTH: God is always honest, dependable, and trustworthy. He wants me to trust His plan for my life and to follow where He leads me.

KEY VERSE: If you keep silent at this time, relief and deliverance will come to the Jewish people from another place, but you and your father's family will be destroyed. Who knows, perhaps you have come to your royal position for such a time as this. Esther 4:14

KEY PASSAGE:
Esther Obeyed God's Plan
(Esther 1–8)

♡ How have I seen God as dependable?

♡ How and when was the last time I completely let go and trusted God?

Read Proverbs 30:5. Pray that the girls you lead will see God as flawless and a place of refuge. As we strive to be brave in a world of unknowns, let's remind ourselves that the more we know God, the more we can trust His plan.

Get Started!

DESIGN A QUEEN

> **YOU WILL NEED:**
> ☐ Item 6: Design a Queen
> ☐ Markers, gel pens, or crayons
> ☐ Stickers, plastic gems (optional)

Give each girl a "Design a Queen" activity sheet. Explain that the goal is to design the best queen she can create. She can draw on the outline and use words to describe what her queen would be like.

After the girls have had time to create their queens, allow them to share their creations. Pay close attention to how many external descriptions they use versus internal descriptions.

Ask: What words did you include on your queen design? Do you think these words would allow those who follow her to trust her in a crazy or difficult circumstance? *(Allow the girls to share.)*

Say: These designs are great! You girls sure are creative. If we are being honest, sometimes when we think of royalty we think of all the outside things like jewels, palaces, and beauty. *(Name other items you saw the girls use to create their queens.)*

Continue: While those things are really nice, no tiara is going to help you stand strong when things get scary, right? Today we are going to hear a Bible story about a queen—Queen Esther. Queen Esther had a fascinating story about bravery. God led Esther to be queen and worked through her to save God's people. Now Esther may have been very beautiful, but it was the way she trusted God that made her brave.

Explain: Sometimes we have ideas that bravery comes from courageous actions, but really bravery starts way before that. Bravery starts not with us, but with God and what we believe to be true about Him. Bravery begins in our hearts and motivations. What we believe to be true about God and what He says about us leads us to take bold and courageous actions that honor God.

Bible Story

Select one girl to be the *queen*. She will stand at one end of the room, facing away from the rest of the group. The other girls will stand at the opposite end of the room and take turns asking for permission to move toward the queen (as in "Mother, May I?").

The queen may grant requests or deny requests and offer alternative options. (E.g., take three hops forward on one foot, take two giant steps forward, take six bunny hops, and so forth.) When the queen offers a different option, the player must comply. When a player reaches the queen, she becomes the next queen. Continue playing until every girl has a turn to be the queen.

Ask: What do you think would make a good queen or a bad queen?

Use a dry erase board or poster board to write down responses.

Say: In today's Bible story, we will learn about an unexpected queen named Esther and how God planned to use her to rescue His people. Esther was selected to be the queen of Persia by the Persian king, Ahasuerus.

Explain: When King Ahasuerus chose Esther to be queen, he didn't make a list of the qualities that make a good queen. He just picked a woman based on her appearance! Thankfully, even in that choice, God was working to protect His people. **God is always honest, dependable, and trustworthy.** In today's Bible story Esther faced a difficult decision to bravely trust God and speak up or to let her fears silence her. Let's read Esther's story and learn more about what it looks like to live as God's brave girl.

Esther Obeyed God's Plan
(ESTHER 1–8)

King Ahasuerus (uh haz yoo EHR uhs) was the king of Persia. Many years earlier, when Cyrus was king, he sent some of God's people back to Judah (the place God's people used to live) to rebuild the temple in Jerusalem. Some of God's people stayed in Persia. God's people were called Jews because they were from Judah. The king of Persia chose Esther to be his queen. Esther didn't tell the king that she was a Jew.

One day, Mordecai (MOR de ki) (Esther's cousin) heard that Haman, an important leader who worked for the king, was planning to kill all the Jews. Mordecai was upset! He was a Jew; he didn't want all the people he loved to be killed. Mordecai and all the Jews cried.

Esther didn't know what was wrong. She sent a messenger to ask Mordecai why all the Jews were upset. Mordecai told Esther about Haman's evil plan.

"You have to do something!" Mordecai said. "Ask the king to stop Haman. Ask him to save the Jewish people."

Esther sent a message back to Mordecai. "No one can approach the king unless the king calls for that person first," Esther said. "The punishment is death— unless the king holds out his scepter; then you may live."

"You're a Jew," Mordecai said. "If you don't stop Haman, he will kill you too. Maybe this is why you are the queen. Maybe God put you in the palace to save the Jewish people!"

Esther asked Mordecai and the Jews not to eat any food for three days, but instead to pray to God. Then Esther would go to the king, even if it meant she might die. On the third day, Esther went to the king. He saw Esther and held out his golden scepter. "What is it, Queen Esther?" the king asked. "What do you want to ask me? I'll give you anything—up to half of my kingdom."

Esther asked, "Would you and Haman come to a feast?"

So Haman, who was planning to kill all the Jews, and the king went to Esther's party. After eating, the king said, "What do you want, Queen Esther? I'll give you anything—up to half of my kingdom."

"Come to my feast again tomorrow," Esther said.

The king agreed. The next day, Haman and the king went to Esther's feast. After eating, the king said, "What do you want, Queen Esther? I'll give you anything—up to half of my kingdom."

Esther spoke up, "There is a plan to kill me and my people." The king replied, "Who is responsible for this plan?" "This evil enemy—Haman!" Esther said.

The king was angry! He punished Haman and made a law to keep the Jewish people safe from their enemies.

Make The Point

Say: Esther's choice to help God's people was not easy. The king had a rule that no one could go to him unless he called for that person. If Esther went to the king without an invitation, he could have her killed. But if the king held out his scepter, that meant he would allow her to live. Esther agreed to help her people, even if it meant she might die.

Explain: Even when life is scary and we are unsure about the future, we can still trust in God. God was working out a plan to use Esther to rescue His people and make the way for His Son, Jesus, to come into the world. **God is always honest, dependable, and trustworthy. He wants us to trust His plan for our lives and to follow where He leads us.** Even when difficult things happen that we can't explain, we can choose to trust God and believe He is in control. That doesn't mean all of our fears or concerns go away. I'm sure Esther was probably still nervous to go before the king, but she trusted God's plan more than her own. That is what bravery looks like. We, too, can take bold actions in our faith because we trust God and believe His plans for us are good.

Bible Study

ALL ABOUT ESTHER

YOU WILL NEED:
- ☐ Study Journals (1 per girl)
- ☐ Bibles (1 per girl)
- ☐ Pens (1 per girl)

TEACHING TIP: Your group is a safe place for your girls. Be sensitive and encouraging to girls who are learning to navigate their Bibles.

Invite the girls to open their journals to "All About Esther" (pg. 20).

Say: Esther was not just an important queen in history. She also had a book in the Bible named after her. Let's see what we can learn about Queen Esther through these passages in the book of the Bible with her name.

Ask: Is the Book of Esther in the Old or New Testament of the Bible? *(Allow girls to guess, but be sensitive to those who are unfamiliar with the Bible.)*

Say: Esther is an Old Testament book, so that means it is in the first part of the Bible. The Book of Esther is right after the Book of Nehemiah and right before the Book of Job. Feel free to use the table of contents in your Bible to find the Book of Esther. Let's practice finding the book, closing our Bibles, and finding it again.

Assist the girls in finding the Book of Esther. When they have all found it, encourage them to close their Bibles and find it again. Do this several times until the girls are more comfortable opening to the Book of Esther.

Give girls time to complete "All about Esther" in their journals and review the answers together.

- ♡ Esther 2:7 — Esther had no **mother** and **father**.
- ♡ Esther 2:7 — Esther was **beautiful**.
- ♡ Esther 2:10 — Esther did not reveal her **ethnicity** or **family background**.

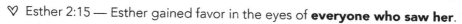

- ♡ Esther 2:15 — Esther gained favor in the eyes of **everyone who saw her**.
- ♡ Esther 4:4 — The queen was overcome with **fear**.
- ♡ Esther 5:2 — As soon as the king saw Esther standing in the courtyard, she gained **favor** with him.
- ♡ Esther 7:3 — "If I have found favor with you, Your Majesty, and if the king is pleased, spare my life; this is my request. And **spare my people**; this is my desire."

Ask: Is there something new that you learned about Esther? What surprised you?

Say: God is always honest, dependable, and trustworthy. He wants us to trust His plan for our lives and to follow where He leads us.

Story Scramble

> **YOU WILL NEED:**
> ☐ Study Journals (1 per girl)
> ☐ Bibles (1 per girl)
> ☐ Pens (1 per girl)

Invite the girls to open their journals to "Story Scramble" (pg. 21). Guide them to complete the statements from today's Bible story. Younger and older girls will fill in the blanks of each statement. Older girls will also number the statements in order. Then they can complete the crossword puzzles with the answers.

- ♡ Mordecai (Esther's uncle) heard that **Haman,** an important leader who worked for the king, was planning to kill all the Jews.
- ♡ Mordecai told Esther that she had to do **something**.
- ♡ Esther was **afraid** to talk to the king about Haman's plan because she could be killed for coming to him.
- ♡ After fasting and praying for **three** days, Esther approached the king.
- ♡ When the **king** saw Esther, he extended his scepter.
- ♡ First, Esther asked for the king and Haman to come to her **feast**.
- ♡ Then, **Esther** revealed Haman's plot after a second feast that she prepared for Haman and the king.
- ♡ When the king heard about Haman's plot, he ordered to have Haman killed and issued a new order to **protect** the Jews and Queen Esther.

Say: It took incredible courage for Esther to approach the king on behalf of her people. She could have been killed, but God used Esther at just the right time to save His people. Isn't it so amazing that God uses ordinary people to accomplish His plan on earth? Esther became a queen, but she didn't start out that way. Esther was just a girl who was willing to let God use her for His purposes. And that's exactly what God did! **He wants us to trust His plan for our lives and to follow where He leads us.**

Small Group Activities

CLING TO GOD

> **YOU WILL NEED:**
> ☐ Pens or pencils for each girl
> ☐ Clear window cling stickers per girl (available at most craft supply stores)
> ☐ Permanent markers of various colors
>
> **TO DO:**
> ☐ Distribute a window cling and a marker to each girl.

Say: We know that God is trustworthy, but we can still have trouble trusting Him at times. Think about a time when it was hard for you to trust God. Maybe something bad or sad happened in your family. Maybe it was hard to trust God when you were stressed with school. Perhaps something big and uncertain happened and you didn't know if God would be with you. After you have thought about a time it was hard for you to trust God, consider how you could pray to God to help you if or when that situation could come up again. Write across the top of your window cling: "Help me trust You when…" Then draw a picture and write words that would encourage you to trust God. For example: Help me trust You when (I am scared, I feel alone, I don't know what to do, I feel sad, and so forth.)

Instruct each child not to write her name on her window cling prayer. Once everyone has finished, invite the girls to place their clings on a window. Challenge them to place their hands on another girl's cling and pray for that girl.

Say: When we need help trusting God, we have to remember who He is. **God is always honest, dependable, and trustworthy. He wants us to trust His plan for our lives and to follow where He leads.**

TRUST WALK

YOU WILL NEED:

☐ Bandana (1 per girl)
☐ Obstacle course items in the meeting space

Invite the girls to help you set up a simple obstacle course using objects nearby. Ask for a volunteer to go first. Blindfold the volunteer and place her on one side of the room. Instruct the other girls to stand on the sides of the room. These girls are to give false instructions on how to make it through the obstacle course.

Explain to the volunteer that she is to listen only to your voice because you will be guiding her through the obstacle course with correct instructions. Call *start* and see how well the volunteer does listening to your instructions over those of the girls misleading her.

Play several rounds allowing each girl a chance to try her way through the obstacle course.

Discuss the following as a group.

Ask:

♡ What was easy or hard about this activity?

♡ Was it difficult to trust the leader's voice to get through the obstacle course?

♡ What was your strategy to get through the obstacle course safely?

Say: In today's lesson, Esther could be brave because she knew and trusted God. **God is always honest, dependable, and trustworthy. He wants me to trust His plan for my life and to follow where He leads me.** We may not be called to stand up for a whole group of people and put our lives on the line like Esther, but there will be times when we are called to bravely trust God's plan.

Pray: Invite the group to pray together, repeating each statement after you either aloud or silently from the prayer below:

Jesus, help us see You for who You are.
When we see You, help us believe.
As we believe, help us look to You to be brave.
We need You, Jesus. Amen.

Conclusion

YOU WILL NEED:
☐ Item 7: Fasting Challenge

TO DO:
☐ Distribute Item 7: Fasting Challenge to each person in the group.

Say: When Esther was faced with a difficult decision, she obeyed God's plan. Esther didn't do this in her own strength. Her bravery came from knowing **God is always honest, dependable, and trustworthy.**

Ask: Let's think back to the Bible story. What did Esther ask for everyone to do while she prepared to bravely follow God's plan. *(Allow the girls to answer.)*

Say: Esther 4:16 says, "Go and assemble all the Jews who can be found in Susa and fast for me. Don't eat or drink for three days, night or day. I and my female servants will also fast in the same way. After that, I will go to the king even if it is against the law. If I perish, I perish." Esther instructed everyone to fast. She knew she could die for going before the king without his permission, but she was willing to do this, even if it meant her own death, so that God's people might be saved.

Ask: How would you describe fasting? *(Allow the girls to answer.)*

Say: Fasting is doing without something to spend more time connecting with God. Esther asked Mordacai, the Jews, and her servants to fast from food and water for three days. They would use the time normally scheduled for eating to spend praying and seeking God. Fasting is a great way to remove distractions so we can focus more on God.

Give the girls a "Focus on God" activity sheet. Explain that they are to cross out things on the paper that keep them from spending time with God. At the blank on the bottom, they are to write what is distracting them from God the most.

After each girl has finished, challenge the group to consider taking the three day reset to eliminate the most distracting item so they can focus on God and spend more time talking to Him.

Make note of who is doing the challenge and encourage them with a note card during the week. Reinforce that we don't do without the distraction just to test ourselves but to spend more time with God.

Say: Esther was a very special woman whom God chose to help save His people. God was with Esther and she bravely trusted God even when she was afraid. Esther prayed and fasted for three days. God heard Esther's prayers and worked through her to save His people.

Explain: The Bible tells us that we are special girls to God, too! God chose us as part of His special plan. He didn't choose us to sit around and do nothing. He chose each of us for a special purpose. God chose you *on* purpose and *for* a purpose. You have a very special reason for being here. You are chosen to reflect God's love and goodness to people around you. This week, consider how you can tune out the most distracting items from your life so you can focus on God and fulfill His purpose for your life of showing God's love to others.

Finish: Girls, I hope you learned something new about God and yourself today. This week, keep exploring who Jesus is and who He made you to be by working through your study journals. Write down any questions or thoughts you may have. Jesus can help you be brave to trust Him this week.

SESSION THREE

Brave to LIVE BOLDLY

Leader Bible Study

When was the last time you have been purely in awe of who God is? Whether you have been a believer for a short time or longer, if we are honest, sometimes we just become too casual with how holy the one true God is.

So today, let us pause. Find a place to block out the world and be still before God. As you prepare to teach about living boldly because God is holy, maybe you need a fresh reminder of His holiness too.

Pray and ask God to open your eyes and reveal Himself to you. Ask Him to show you just how set apart He is and remind you of His holy presence in your life.

Open your Bible to Isaiah 6. Even if this passage is familiar to you, take time to read each word aloud. Pause when you need to. Underline or highlight phrases that stand out to you. Read through this passage at least once and then just sit in God's presence, reflect, and pray. When you are finished, pause to worship God by reading or singing through the hymn.

HOLY, HOLY, HOLY

Holy, holy, holy!
Lord God Almighty
Early in the morning
Our song shall rise
to Thee

Holy, holy, holy!
Merciful and mighty
God in three Persons
Blessed Trinity!

Holy, holy, holy!
Though the darkness
hide thee / Though
the eye of sinful man
Thy glory may not see

Only Thou art holy
There is none beside
Thee / Perfect in power,
in love and purity

Holy, holy, holy!
Lord God Almighty
Oh thy works shall praise
Thy name / In earth and
sky and sea

Holy, holy, holy!
Merciful and mighty
God in three Persons
Blessed Trinity!

Get Started!

The Perfect Square

YOU WILL NEED:
- ☐ Blindfolds (1 per girl)
- ☐ A long rope or yarn
- ☐ Yard stick (optional)

TEACHING TIP: For younger girls, consider allowing them to complete the task without blindfolds. The girls will likely not be able to completely make a perfect square. If it looks close, be sure to point out small mistakes or imperfect angles. If time allows, measure each side to see if it is exactly equal.

Gather the group into a circle. Blindfold each player and give her part of the rope or yarn to hold in a circle. Explain that when you say *go* the group will work together to move from their circle to a perfect square and lay the rope or yarn down on the floor into the shape of a perfect square. (For additional rounds you can add triangle, diamond, and so forth.) Once the girls have completed the task, invite them to remove their blindfolds and see how well they did.

Ask: What made this activity easy or hard? *(Allow the girls to answer. Help them see that, due to their limitations, it was really impossible for them to be perfect.)*

Say: You might have thought at the beginning that this was an easy task, but if we're honest, we are nowhere near perfect, are we? No matter how hard we try, we will always fall short. We'll never be perfect. Now before you get too upset about that, let me remind you that God is holy and perfect. **Through Jesus, we can follow God and pattern our lives after Him.** There is hope for us in Jesus. Today we will look at a Bible story where someone came face to face with the holiness of God. Let's pay close attention to how this person reacted and what he learned about himself.

Bible Story

YOU WILL NEED:

☐ Several household or classroom items (spoon, book, clock, towel, pencil, pillow, and so forth)
☐ Study Journals (1 per girl)
☐ Markers or crayons

Collect a variety of common household or classroom objects and display three or four items at a time. Challenge the girls to share what the items have in common. Then instruct them to list what is different about the items. Affirm the girls' observations. Then show three or four different items and play again.

Say: In today's Bible story, God is called "holy, holy holy." The word *holy* means "set apart." How do you think God is set apart or different from us? (*Allow the girls to respond.*)

Say: A prophet named Isaiah was chosen by God to give a special message to God's people. During this time a man named Uzziah was the king of Judah. He was mostly a good king, but he wasn't perfect. King Uzziah had just died and the people were worried and afraid. Who would lead them now that their good king was gone?

Continue: We're going to see today how being in the presence of God changed Isaiah's perspective and led him to take bold actions. Today we are going to consider how God calls us to live boldly because we are called daughters of the King. God is the King over everything! Because of who God is, we can have confidence to follow Him with boldness and certainty.

Invite the girls to open their study journals to "Set Apart" (p. 32). Explain that as you tell today's Bible story, each girl will listen closely and draw what she hears about in the Bible story. Inform the group that you will go through the story slowly so that they can hear and take time to imagine and draw what the scene may have looked like.

The Holiness of God
(ISAIAH 6)

In the year that King Uzziah died, Isaiah (a prophet) was worshiping God in the temple when he had a vision. Isaiah saw God sitting on a throne. God's robe was long; its edges filled the temple. Seraphim—heavenly beings—stood above Him, and they each had six wings. They called out: "Holy, holy, holy is the Lord; His glory fills the whole earth."

When the seraphim spoke, the foundations of the doorways shook, and the temple filled with smoke. Isaiah was in the presence of God!

He said, "I am ruined! I am sinful. I do not deserve to be in the presence of the King, the great and holy God."

Then one of the seraphim flew to Isaiah. The seraph (heavenly being) had a burning coal from the altar in his hand. He touched Isaiah's mouth and said, "Now that this has touched your lips, your wickedness is removed and your sin is wiped away."

Then Isaiah heard God's voice: "Who should I send? Who will go for Us?"

Isaiah said, "Here am I! Send me."

"Go," God said.

God told Isaiah an important message for the people. This was God's message: "You will listen, but you will not understand. You will look, but you will not really see. If your eyes and ears and minds worked, you would turn from your sin and be healed." Isaiah asked, "How long should I preach to people who won't listen?"

God answered Isaiah, "Preach until the cities are destroyed and no one lives in them. I am going to send the people far away."

Then God explained that He would bring some of the people back to Judah. These people were part of Abraham's family. God was going to keep His promise to Abraham through them. He would send the Messiah through their family to be a blessing to all the nations.

MAKE THE POINT

Say: Isaiah saw the holy God in His glory, and it changed his life forever. When he learned something new about God, his thinking was changed and he realized how sinful he was. God forgave Isaiah. Like Isaiah, when we see how holy God is, we see how sinful we are. The good news is that God sent His Son, Jesus, to take away our sin. We can turn to Him and be forgiven of the wrong things we've done and trust in Him as our good King.

Explain: You might think that asking for forgiveness and making bold choices don't go together. After all, when you ask for forgiveness, you usually feel bad about what you've done. But we learn from Isaiah that it is God's forgiveness and grace that leads to bold living! When we trust in Jesus, He changes us and we are called daughters of God. Because God makes us new, we can live in bold confidence to follow Him and pattern our lives after Him. We are brave not because of who we are on our own but because of who God is and how He changes us. God promises to always be with us. He gives us the strength and courage to face any situation because we are forgiven and called His daughters.

Bible Study

SET APART

> **YOU WILL NEED:**
> ☐ Study Journals (1 per girl)
> ☐ Chair
> ☐ Decorations to make the chair look like a throne (optional)

After you read the Bible story, allow the girls time to draw about what they heard. Invite those who feel comfortable to share their drawings.

♡ What stood out to you most in this passage of Scripture? *(Allow the girls to share, and be prepared to share what stood out to you most as well.)*

♡ How do you imagine you would have responded if you were Isaiah?

♡ How would you explain the word *holy*?

Say: We heard the word *holy* repeated in today's Bible story several times. The visual this passage gives us can help us understand the true meaning of the word *holy*. Let's take a closer look at a similar visual now.

Ask for five volunteers. Guide one volunteer to sit on one side of the room in a chair. If possible, make the chair look more like a throne by decorating it or placing it higher than a typical chair. Invite three of the volunteers to stand behind the chair and when instructed, guide them to repeat "holy, holy, holy" over and over. Place the fifth volunteer near the chair.

Ask:

♡ Let's look at our volunteer on the throne. Who do you think she represents? *(God)*

♡ Now let's turn our eyes to our other volunteer who represents Isaiah. As I read Isaiah 6:5 again, let's imagine his posture as we see his response. *(Invite the girls to share their opinions.)*

♡ Are God and Isaiah equals? Why or why not? *(Allow the girls to share their responses.)*

Say: God and Isaiah were not the same at all. We see that by how Isaiah reacted. God is set apart from Isaiah. That's what it means to be holy—to be set apart. God is holy and perfect, and we are sinful like Isaiah, but there is hope. Isaiah recognized the wrong things he had done and confessed them to God.

Read Romans 3:23; Romans 6:23.

Ask: How does this truth from God's Word help you understand that God is holy and perfect?

Say: Through Jesus alone we have hope and can be transformed, or made new. When we receive Jesus as Savior, we can pattern our lives after Him with the help of the Holy Spirit who lives inside us.

WHAT IS WORSHIP?

Say: Followers of God know there is one source for their strength and bravery—God Himself. As God's brave girl, you need to understand there is only One worthy of worship.

Ask: How would you explain worship to someone? (*Allow the girls to respond.*) Is worship just singing? Why or why not?

Guide the girls to open their journals to "What Is Worship?" (pg. 33). Remind them that in today's Bible story, we learned that Isaiah was worshiping God when he had an unforgettable encounter. Help the girls understand how worship can also be part of their daily lives.

Say: Let's complete the definition of worship in your journals. Worship comes from an old word *worthship* that means something we assign worth to. So to worship means *to assign proper worth and deep respect to God.* Worship can happen on your own and with other people. It is not just singing songs, although that is part of it. Let's look at four ways we can worship God.

Continue: In the first square write *reading the Bible.* In this square write what is easy or hard for you about reading the Bible. (*Allow the girls to share.*) Then write what time of day works best for you to read the Bible. A routine is so helpful.

Say: In the second square write *singing.* Do you have a favorite worship song to sing? Write the name of it in that box. Then write where you like to sing to God.

Continue: In the third box write *praying.* How many times a week do you think you pray? Write that number in the box. Now write what you wish that number was. Now you have a goal. Where is a special place you can get alone and pray to God? Draw something that represents that place in the box.

Say: In the last box write *preaching.* Now you may not be a preacher, but it is so important that we worship God through hearing His Word preached. Do you have a favorite preacher or Bible teacher? Write that name in the box. Also write one thing you have learned from a preacher or Bible teacher.

Small Group Activities

Here I Am

Ask for a volunteer to go first and be the *caller*. Place her on one side of the room with her back to the rest of the group. Silently choose one person to be *Isaiah*. Instruct *Isaiah* to mingle and walk around the room with the rest of the kids.

When the *caller* asks "Who will go?" *Isaiah* will answer "Here I am, send me!" Encourage *Isaiah* to try and disguise her voice so the caller will not recognize her.

After *Isaiah* replies, allow a couple more seconds for the group to mingle around the room. Invite the *caller* to turn around and try to guess who was *Isaiah* in that round. Play several rounds allowing different kids to play the part of the *caller* and *Isaiah*.

Say: In this activity the *caller* was like God in our Bible story. Several of you got to play the part of Isaiah. This activity is a reminder to us that through Jesus we can follow God and we should be ready to answer His call to go and do what, as believers, He calls us to do.

No Sew DIY Scrunchies

YOU WILL NEED:
- ☐ Item 8: Scrunchie Pattern
- ☐ Examples of clothing patterns (available in most craft stores or online)
- ☐ Tape
- ☐ Various pieces of fabric 4-by-22 inch (⅛ yard = 2 scrunchies)
- ☐ Markers or pens
- ☐ Scissors
- ☐ 10 inch elastic strips per girl (¼ inch or ½ inch)
- ☐ Safety pins (1 per girl)
- ☐ Hot glue gun and glue sticks

Display an example of a clothing pattern from a fabric store. Explain how important a pattern is when making multiple copies of the same garment. Help the girls understand that the pattern is the blueprint of how a piece of clothing will look once it is complete. Discuss the following with your group.

Ask:

♡ How important is the pattern in making copies of a piece of clothing? *(The pattern is the standard for what the garment is going to look like. Without the pattern the garment might not turn out like it is supposed to.)*

♡ Who are we supposed to pattern our lives after? *(We are called to pattern our lives after God because He made us to reflect Him.* **God is holy and perfect. Through Jesus, we can follow God and pattern our lives after Him.***)*

Say: Let's make some fun scrunchies with a sewing pattern to help remind us of the importance of patterning our lives after Jesus.

Distribute a "Scrunchie Pattern" to each girl and explain the directions listed. Instruct the girls to cut apart the pattern by cutting along its edges. Next, demonstrate how to tape the two ends of the pattern together, so that the girls each end up with a 4 x 22 inch pattern. Then, lead the girls to choose a piece of fabric, trace the pattern onto the wrong side of the fabric with a pencil or pen, and cut it out.

Next, ask an adult leader to add a line of hot glue to the wrong side edge of the short ends of each piece of fabric. Guide the girls to quickly fold the edges of fabric over the glue to seal the ends of the fabric.

Once the glue is dry, instruct the girls to fold the fabric in half lengthwise, with the pattern on the inside. Place a bead of glue along the outer edge of one side of fabric and place the other side on top of it. Working in sections, continue gluing the outer edge all the way down, creating a tube.

Invite the girls to turn their tubes right-side out using a safety pin as a guide. Distribute the 10-inch pieces of elastic and guide the girls to fasten the safety pin on one side. Insert the elastic strip into the tube, using the safety pin to weave the elastic through the fabric. Once the elastic is inside the tube, tie the ends in a knot.

To finish the scrunchie, slide one end of the fabric tube into the other end. Secure the ends of fabric together with hot glue.

Say: Your scrunchies look great! Imagine what they would look like if we didn't have a pattern to follow. Every time you look at your scrunchies you can be reminded that **God is holy and perfect. Through Jesus, we can follow God and pattern our lives after Him.**

Conclusion

YOU WILL NEED:
- ☐ Item 3: Allergy Alert
- ☐ Hand mirrors (1 per girl)
- ☐ Petroleum jelly
- ☐ Cotton swab (1 per girl)
- ☐ Tissues
- ☐ Bowl of warm water
- ☐ Dish soap
- ☐ Bowl of vinegar water (equal parts water and vinegar)
- ☐ Two sponges

ALLERGY ALERT: Girls will be using petroleum jelly. Please make sure there are no girls with this allergy in your class.

Say: In today's lesson, Isaiah's response to standing before a holy God was this: "Woe is me for I am ruined because I am a man of unclean lips and live among a people of unclean lips, and because my eyes have seen the King, the LORD of Armies" (Isaiah 6:5).

When Isaiah came face to face with God, he could clearly see his sin. Sometimes it is harder for us to see our sin.

Hand each participant a mirror and a cotton swab. Pass the petroleum jelly around the group instructing each girl to dip the cotton swab in the petroleum jelly, and then put some on her lips like lip gloss.

Say: While looking at yourself in the mirror, take a moment and think about ways you may have had a bad attitude, been hurtful with your words, gossiped, told a lie, or disrespected your parents before. As you think of each of these, kiss the mirror in front of you.

Ask: As you look in the mirror, what are your thoughts? How does seeing your "unclean lips" on the mirror in front of you help you understand your sinfulness?

Say: I am going to hand each of you a tissue and I want you to clean your mirror.

Allow the girls to try to clean their mirrors with just a tissue.

Say: You probably noticed that there is no way for you to get your mirror clean on your own. Would you like some help?

Guide the girls to first put dish soap on their mirrors and then to scrub it off in the soapy water bowl. Next invite them to dip their mirrors in the vinegar bowl to get off any remaining residue.

Say: When we recognize our wrong choices compared to a holy and perfect God, we know that we are not holy like God. There is nothing we can do to clean ourselves up or try to fix our sin problem. Like with cleaning the mirrors, we need help. We cannot get rid of our sin on our own.

Finish: Girls, it is a victory when we realize we need help. Jesus came to take the punishment for our sin. When we trust in Jesus, we can stand in confidence knowing that because of Jesus, God doesn't see us as sinful. He sees us as He sees Jesus—perfect. **God is holy and perfect. Through Jesus, we can follow God and pattern our lives after Him.** This week, keep exploring who Jesus is and who He made you to be by working through your study journals. Write down any questions or thoughts you may have. Jesus can help you bravely trust Him this week.

SESSION FOUR

Brave to LOVE FIERCELY

Leader Bible Study

Love in our culture is tricky, especially with girls. Girls might see love thrown around like a game or a bargaining chip. They might see love cheapened or distorted into something it was never intended to be. The girls you lead may have experienced trauma or life situations that have led them to distrust and reject genuine love. As you prepare to teach this lesson, pause and remind yourself about the love of your heavenly Father. His love is so much more than what the world offers.

God loves and values all people. That means God loves you. We hear that and even teach that, but it is important to remind ourselves of this truth and experience His love in our lives in fresh ways.

Find and read the following verses in your Bible. If you mark in your Bible, make a note in the margin with a heart that these Scriptures remind us of God's love.

- ♡ 1 John 4:9-10
- ♡ John 3:16
- ♡ Romans 8:38-39
- ♡ John 15:9
- ♡ Romans 5:8
- ♡ Ephesians 2:4-5

How would you describe the love of God?

Write the names of each girl in your group in the hearts below. (If needed put two names in each heart.) Pray over each name. Ask God to open the eyes of these girls to His love that is beyond comprehension. Pray that as they experience and are changed by His love, they will love others like He loves them.

Get Started!

VALUABLE TREASURES

YOU WILL NEED:
- ☐ Hand mirrors
- ☐ Sticky notes (3 per girl)
- ☐ Pens (1 per girl)
- ☐ Masking tape

TO DO:
- ☐ Tape a cross in a large space in the room. Girls will sit in a circle around the cross shape.

Give the girls three sticky notes and a pen. Challenge them to think of three possessions they have that mean a lot to them. Some examples may be an electronic, their home, a toy, and so forth. Invite them to write one item on each sticky note. After they have finished, guide the girls to sit in a circle around the cross shape and place all three sticky notes out in front of them. Then, explain that everyone will need to choose one item to give away. Instruct the girls to choose from their three notes which one they will give up. Repeat this exercise so that the girls are left with only one sticky note.

Ask: Why have you held onto this note? *(Allow the girls to share.)* Imagine someone asked you to give that item up. How hard would it be for you to give that up? *(Allow the girls to share.)*

Say: Let's pretend that Jesus is coming to town and you want to present Him with a gift. What if the item in front of you, your most valuable possession, is the only thing you have to give Him?

Guide the girls to pause for a minute and really think through the cost of giving that gift to Jesus. Invite them, if and when they are ready, to take that sticky note and place it on the cross as a symbol of giving it to Jesus.

Say: This activity may have been easy or difficult for you. Today, we will see how a woman used her costly gift to worship Jesus.

Bible Story

Say: We can use our five senses to learn about God through His creation. We can also use a few of those senses to explore God's Word. That's what we will be doing today! The sense of smell is one of our strongest memory makers.

Before the session, prepare several containers of scents.

Form two groups. Instruct the groups to send one player at a time to smell a scent. The player should report to her group what she smelled. Groups should identify the scents and list their guesses on a piece of paper. Groups may choose to send additional players to confirm a scent. Call on the groups to share their guesses. Then reveal the actual scents.

Ask: Which of these scents did you like? Were there any scents you didn't like?

Say: Today we are going to hear a story from the Bible about a woman who gave up a costly gift and poured sweet-smelling oil on Jesus. Let's find out why.

Jesus Was Anointed
(MATTHEW 26:6-13; MARK 14:3-9; JOHN 12:1-8)

The time was coming to celebrate the Passover. Every year, the Jewish people gathered together to remember a special event that happened long ago. When God's people were slaves in Egypt, God did great things to rescue His people. The pharaoh saw God's power and authority, and the pharaoh let God's people go. God had used Moses to lead His people out of Egypt and to the promised land. God did not want the people to forget that time, so every year, the Jews had a feast. Many Jews traveled to Jerusalem to celebrate.

Six days before the Passover feast began, Jesus went to the town of Bethany. Bethany was near Jerusalem, and Jesus' friend Lazarus lived there with his sisters, Mary and Martha.

Jesus went to His friend Simon's house for a meal. Jesus was reclining at the table when Lazarus's sister Mary came to Him. She had a jar of very expensive oil. The oil smelled good, like a perfume. Mary broke open the jar and poured the oil on Jesus' head and feet.

Jesus' disciples were very upset! They thought Mary had wasted the expensive oil by pouring it on Jesus. The oil was worth 300 denarii—about a year's pay. One of the disciples, Judas Iscariot (iss KAR ih aht), said, "She could have sold the oil for a lot of money, and then she could have given the money to the poor!" Judas did not say this because he cared about the poor; he said it because he loved money. In fact, he was a thief.

They told Mary that she had done the wrong thing, but Jesus spoke up. "Leave her alone," He said. "She has done a very good thing for Me."

Then Jesus explained, "You will always have people around you who are poor, but you will not always have Me. Mary has poured oil on My body to get it ready for burial."

Jesus said that wherever the gospel was told in the whole world, people would also hear about Mary and what she had done.

MAKE THE POINT

Say: The perfume that Mary poured on Jesus was no doubt precious to her, but she gave it all to Jesus. She believed Jesus was more valuable than her costly perfume. Mary's actions demonstrated a fierce love for Jesus. She showed others that Jesus deserves to be honored and worshiped.

Explain: Pouring the expensive oil on Jesus was not a waste; it was worship. By allowing Mary to anoint Him, Jesus showed that He is more valuable than anything. Jesus knew that He would soon die on the cross, be buried, and rise again on the third day. Mary's fierce love for Jesus is important for us to remember, but it is very small compared to Jesus' great love for us. Jesus paid the consequences for every one of our wrong actions, thoughts, words, and motivations. He died for us because of His extravagant love for us. Because of Jesus' love for us, we can love and worship God and love others with a fierce, never-giving-up kind of love. **God loves and values all people. He calls us to live bravely and love like He loves.**

Bible Study

VALUING ALL PEOPLE

> **YOU WILL NEED:**
> ☐ Study Journals (1 per girl)
> ☐ Pens (1 per girl)

Say: Today we are learning that God loves and values all people. He calls us to live bravely and love like He loves. As we think about the Bible story, let's look honestly at how we love one another.

Invite the girls to look at "Valuing All People" in their journals (pg. 44). Explain that the only way to grow as God's brave girls is to be honest about where we are now. When we see where we have room to grow, we can move forward to live and love more like Jesus. Give the girls time to complete their questionnaires and explain that what they write is for their eyes only. Be prepared to help the girls answer questions if they are struggling.

♡ Someone that is hard for me to love is _____.
  (You can write his or her initials.)

♡ Someone I need to include more with my friends is _____.

♡ I have been guilty of gossiping about someone.
  YES   NO   I'M NOT SURE

♡ A friend I need to invite to church is _____.

♡ I have made fun of someone before.
  YES   NO   I'M NOT SURE

♡ Are there people I treat differently because they don't look like me?
  YES   NO   I'M NOT SURE

♡ I am a safe person that friends can share secrets with.
  YES   NO   I'M NOT SURE

♡ A person's heart is more important to me than how she looks or dresses.
  YES   NO   I'M NOT SURE

♡ I look for people that need a friend.
  YES   NO   I'M NOT SURE

♡ I am brave and stand up for people when no one else will.
  YES   NO   I'M NOT SURE

♡ I am brave and stand up for Jesus.
  YES   NO   I'M NOT SURE

Say: Girls, sometimes it can be hard to love like God does. If it were easy it wouldn't take brave girls to do it. In today's Bible story, we read about a woman who refused to worry about what others thought or said about her. She loved Jesus so much, she couldn't help but show it. She was truly brave and loved like God loves. Her story reminds us of God's great love for us and how we can love Him and others fiercely and bravely. We love others because of God's love for us.

Passage Comparison

YOU WILL NEED:
☐ Study Journals (1 per girl)
☐ Pens (1 per girl)

Lead the girls to form small groups. Explain that this passage about Mary anointing Jesus is found in three places in the Bible—Matthew, Mark, and John.

Instruct each group to open their journals to "Passage Comparison" (pg. 45).

Say: We are going to look at all three of the accounts of this true story of Mary anointing Jesus' feet. They will be a bit different because they are told by three different people: Matthew, Mark, and John. If three of us witnessed the same event, we would explain it differently. These men each shared different details or focused on different aspects of this amazing, true story.

Guide the groups to find and read all three passages in their Bibles. Then, allow time for the girls to write down the similarities and differences. Explain to the girls that a great Bible study practice is to compare true accounts that are shared in different places in the Bible. Take time for the groups to share what they learned.

Ask:

♥ What was Jesus' response to this brave act of love?

♥ What was brave about Mary's act of love?

♥ What do we know about how Jesus loves?

♥ What about this Bible study activity made the biggest impression on you?

Say: Aren't we glad that God loves all people? No matter who you are, how much money you have, how many times you mess up—God loves and values everyone—including you! Because Mary experienced God's love in Jesus, she was able to bravely love Him back. Mary didn't worry about what other people were thinking. Just like Mary, God calls us to live bravely and love like He loves.

Ask: Is there anything that is keeping you from bravely loving others like God loves you? *(Allow the girls to really be open here. After they share, close this time praying for each of them by name to know God's love and bravely share it with others.)*

Small Group Activities

HOMEMADE PERFUME

YOU WILL NEED:

- ☐ Item 3: Allergy Alert
- ☐ Small glass roll-on bottles (1 per girl) (available at most craft stores)
- ☐ Fractionated coconut oil (available at most craft stores)
- ☐ Small liquid measuring cups
- ☐ Various fragrant essential oils
- ☐ Paper bowls (1 per girl)
- ☐ Several droppers
- ☐ Plastic spoons (1 per girl)
- ☐ Small labels (1 per girl)
- ☐ Markers

TO DO:

- ☐ Post the allergy alert listing the ingredients.

TEACHING TIP: Search online for various complementary oil combinations.

Gather all the supplies on the table. Give each girl a bowl and an empty bottle.

Say: Today you will get to create your very own perfume. Think about what smells you want in your perfume. As you create your perfume, think about how the perfume oil that Mary brought to Jesus was very expensive.

Instruct the girls to measure out ten milliliters of oil into their paper bowls. After they decide on two or three oils to add, lead them to drop ten total drops of oil into their bowls (e.g. four drops of peppermint, three drops of lavender, and three drops of orange). Guide the girls to mix their ingredients in their provided bowls. Once they have their scents completed, guide them to add the mixture to their bottles using a dropper and place the roller and lid on tightly.

Once their perfume is in their bottles, instruct the group to name their perfumes based on today's lesson. Let them brainstorm creative perfume names and then design perfume labels to place on their bottles. Allow the girls to share their scents, names, and the reasons behind their perfumes' name.

BLESSING BAGS

YOU WILL NEED:

- ☐ Gallon ziplock bags (1 per girl)
- ☐ Small bottled water (1 per bag)
- ☐ Granola bars (1 per bag)
- ☐ Adult socks (1 per bag)
- ☐ Travel wipes packages (1 per bag)
- ☐ Other items as needed
- ☐ Construction paper
- ☐ Markers

TEACHING TIP: To aid in the collecting of supplies, assign items for class members to bring the week before. Send reminders throughout the week in case anyone forgets to bring their item.

Say: God loves and values all people. He calls us to live bravely and love like He loves. Because God loves all people, we are going to make some blessing bags to love those who often get overlooked—people experiencing homelessness. We have a lot of love that we can share with others. Let's share God's love and be a blessing to others at the same time.

Give each girl a gallon ziplock bag. Instruct the group to carefully pack each item into their bags. After they have packed their items, invite them to make a card for a person experiencing homelessness. Discuss different Bible verses about God's love they can include on their cards. On that card they should boldly and bravely share how God loves the person who will receive the bag.

After the girls have finished, instruct them to fold their cards and put them in the bags. Invite the girls to hold their bags in their laps as you pray over them.

Pray: *God, You love us so big, and You value all people. Help us boldly and bravely share Your love with someone in need. We trust that You will show us the right moment and person to give these bags to. In Jesus' name, amen.*

Share with the girls that they will keep their blessing bags in their family's vehicle and when they pass someone on the street in need, with the help of an adult, they can hand that person the blessing bag.

Conclusion

YOU WILL NEED:
- ☐ Item 9: Love Coupons (1 sheet per girl)
- ☐ Markers
- ☐ Scissors

TO DO:
- ☐ Print Item 9: Love Coupons

Ask: Do you ever want to share God's love but get nervous that you won't do it right or may mess up? *(Allow the girls to respond and discuss.)*

Say: One way to become better at loving bravely like God does is to make a plan.

Distribute the "Love Coupons" to each girl along with scissors and markers.

Continue: Look at your coupons that you have colored and cut apart. On each coupon there is a compliment (Do you know how big God loves you?) or free task (Because I love you, I will empty the dishwasher.) Think through who in your life needs to receive these coupons. Don't just play it safe. Think about people who really need to experience the love of God, not just people you know would like to receive a coupon.

Guide girls in cutting out the coupons and coloring them. Encourage the group to time to fill in the names of people they want to share their coupons with in the "To" blank. Allow the girls time to address their coupons to people in their lives who need to experience God's love.

Say: Remember, you don't have to be perfect to bravely love like God does. You just have to trust God and let Him lead your actions. Let's spend time praying for the people who will receive our coupons, asking God to help us be brave. Hold one your coupons in your hands in front of you. We will each take a turn to pray the following prayer:

God help me be brave to love all people like You do. Give me the courage to give a coupon to _____.

After each person has prayed aloud, close the group in prayer.

Pray: *God we know only You love perfectly, and You empower us to love others like You do. Will You take our fears and replace them with courage so we can love bravely? In Jesus' name, amen.*

Finish: Girls, I hope you were reminded about God's love for you today. Because of His love for us, we can receive His love and love others around us with that same fierce love. This week, keep exploring who Jesus is and who He made you to be by working through your study journals. Write down any questions or thoughts you may have. Jesus can help you bravely trust Him and love others this week.

Brave to PRAY FEARLESSLY

Leader Bible Study

Prayer is a big part of drawing closer to God and getting to know Him more. As you prepare to teach, take a moment to pray using the CHAT method of prayer you will teach your group at the end of this session. Ask God to prepare your heart and to remind you how much He loves to talk and listen to His girls.

Cheer

Think about how great our God is. God has not forgotten who He is, but we often do. Take time to audibly praise God for who He is in your life right now.

Humble Yourself

Silently confess your sins before God. Ask Him to show you your sin clearly and how it affects your relationship with Him. Agree with God that it is sin.

Appreciate What God Has Done

God has done so much for us, and we have much to be thankful for. Hold your hands out in front of you and imagine that you are holding something God has provided for you. Spend time thanking God for His provision.

Tell God Your Needs

God knows us and our needs better than we know ourselves. Looking at your open hands, pray to God and give Him your fears and worries. Give Him your family and friends who are in need. Pray for the girls in your group by name, asking Him to raise up fearless prayer warriors in this group.

KEY TRUTH:

Prayer is talking and listening to God. When we pray we can praise God, ask Him for help, and confess sin to Him. God wants us to pray to Him, confident that He hears and answers our prayers.

KEY VERSE:

And Mary said: "My soul magnifies the Lord." Luke 1:46

KEY PASSAGE:

Mary's Prayer: (Luke 1:46-55)

Get Started!

ALPHABET PRAISE

Gather the girls in a circle. Explain that they are going to start today's session by praising God.

Say: Prayer is a big part of learning about God and getting to know Him personally. One way that we can pray to God is by praising Him. When we praise God, we are giving Him honor for who He is. Praise is different than thanking God for what He has done. When we praise Him we are praising Him for who He is, acknowledging what is true about His character. We can praise God because He is kind, holy, powerful, loving, and so much more.

Continue: I hope you have your creative minds ready because we are going to praise God through the alphabet. I will say a letter and if you know of something God is that begins with that letter, step forward, and I will call on you to say, "God I praise You because You are…"

Go through the alphabet in order. For example, when you call *A*, the girls may say things like, "God, I praise You because You are awesome. God, I praise You because You are amazing." You may have to give extra time and ideas for certain letters, but allow the girls some time to think through all the characteristics of who God is. Allow creative suggestions for difficult letters (e.g., *Q*: quite amazing, *X*: extraordinarily, *Z*: zealous, and so forth).

Bible Story

YOU WILL NEED:
- [ ] 4 sheets of paper with one of these names on each of them: *Jesus, Paul, David,* and *Jonah*
- [ ] Bible (1 per girl)

TO DO:
- [ ] Write one of the four names on each of the sheets of paper and hang one in each corner of the room.

Say: Today we will hear about one girl's prayer after some pretty shocking news. But before we hear it, let's dig a little deeper into the Bible and see some other prayers by brave followers of God.

Encourage the girls to turn to each prayer in the Bible. Give the girls tips for finding each prayer and show them how to use the table of contents to find prayers in hard-to-find Bible books. Invite one girl to read the prayer aloud. Then give the girls ten seconds to choose the corner with the name that they believe prayed that prayer. Help them see context clues in the Bible.

♡ John 17:1-5 (Jesus) — Before His crucifixion, Jesus was praying in the garden that God would be glorified.

♡ Psalm 51 (David) — David was repenting in the prayer. That means he was agreeing with God about his sin and turning away from sin back to God.

♡ Philippians 1:3-11 (Paul) — Paul was praying for the Philippian church.

♡ Jonah 2 (Jonah) — Jonah prayed this prayer from the belly of a big fish. He had disobeyed God big time and found himself in trouble.

♡ Matthew 6:5-15 (Jesus) — This is called the Lord's Prayer. Jesus used it to teach people how to pray.

Say: Remember, **prayer is talking and listening to God. When we pray to God we can praise Him, ask Him for help, and confess sin to Him.**

Ask: Which prayer spoke to you most and why? What did you learn about prayer through them? How do these prayers help you be confident that God hears and answers your prayers? *(Allow the girls to respond and discuss.)*

Say: Today, we are going to open our Bibles to learn about a woman who praised God through prayer after she found out some surprising news. Let's read today's Bible story to find out what happened.

Mary's Prayer
(LUKE 1:46-55)

One day, God sent an angel named Gabriel to a town called Nazareth. The angel went to visit a young virgin named Mary. She was engaged to be married to Joseph, a descendant of King David. The angel said to Mary, "Rejoice! You have found favor with God. He is with you." Mary was very afraid and puzzled. Why would God find favor with her? She had done nothing special.

"Do not be afraid," the angel said. Then he told Mary that she was going to have a very special and unique baby, and they would call the baby Jesus, which means "the Lord saves." The angel explained that the baby would be great—He would be God's Son! He would even be a king—the king God promised would come.

Mary asked the angel, "How can that happen? I am not married yet." The angel replied, "God will be the father of the baby. The baby will be God's Son."

Then the angel told Mary, "Nothing will be impossible with God!" He said that Mary's relative Elizabeth was pregnant, even though she was old and did not have any children. "May everything happen just as you said," Mary replied. Then the angel left her.

Mary hurried to her relative Elizabeth's house. When she arrived, the baby inside Elizabeth leaped for joy! The Holy Spirit filled Elizabeth and she said, "What an honor, Mary! Your baby will be blessed too!"

Mary was so happy. She praised God with a song about how great God is. Her song went like this:

My soul praises the greatness of the Lord, and my spirit rejoices in God my Savior, because He has looked with favor on the humble condition of His servant. Surely, from now on all generations will call me blessed, because the Mighty One has done great things for me, and His name is holy. His mercy is from generation to generation on those who fear Him. He has done a mighty deed with His arm; He has scattered the proud because of the thoughts of their hearts; He has toppled the mighty from their thrones and exalted the lowly. He has satisfied the hungry with good things and sent the rich away empty. He has helped His servant Israel, remembering His mercy to Abraham and His descendants forever, just as He spoke to our ancestors.

MAKE THE POINT

Say: Mary had her world turned upside down. She went from being a quiet Jewish girl, who no one knew, to being chosen to be the mother of Jesus. She may have been really anxious, worried, or scared, but Mary's response demonstrated her faith in God. Mary prayed fearlessly because she was confident that God heard her. Mary's confidence didn't come from herself. She was just a young teenage girl. Her confidence didn't come from her circumstances. Mary's confidence came in who she knew God to be. Because of her certainty in who God is, she knew He heard her praise.

Continue: Girls, God has created you to pray fearlessly. He wants us to talk to Him when we are thankful, happy, nervous, anxious, appreciative, scared, and even angry. No matter what we are feeling, we can turn to God and have confidence that He hears us and He wants to talk to us. **Prayer is talking and listening to God. When we pray we can praise God, ask Him for help, and confess sin to Him. God wants us to pray to Him, confident that He hears and answers our prayers.**

Bible Study

MARY'S PRAYER

YOU WILL NEED:
- ☐ Study Journals (1 per girl)
- ☐ Highlighters (1 per girl)
- ☐ Blank name tags (1 per girl)
- ☐ Markers (1 per girl)

Invite the girls to open their journals to "Mary's Prayer" (pg. 56). Give the girls highlighters and instruct them to read over Mary's prayer of praise several times. Invite the girls to highlight words that Mary used in her prayer to describe God. After they have highlighted these words, guide them to circle the description of God that meant the most to them.

After each girl has finished, circle up and discuss what they learned about God.

Ask:

- ♡ What were some things we learned about who God is from Mary's prayer?
- ♡ How did Mary's knowledge of such things help her pray boldly during a really crazy time?
- ♡ Which words used to describe God meant the most to you and why?
- ♡ Which description of God would you like to experience in your life this week and why?

After the discussion, hand each girl a name tag and a marker. Instruct the girls to write the following on their name tags, "I can pray fearlessly to God because He is…" and have them fill in the blank with the description that meant the most to them in Mary's prayer. Instruct them to place the name tags on their shirts as a reminder that God hears their prayers.

Say: Prayer is talking and listening to God. You don't have to use fancy words or pray perfect prayers. God knows your heart and what is on your mind. He just wants you to trust Him enough to talk to Him about it. God wants you to communicate Him. Think about talking to God like you would share all that is going on in your life with a close friend. Mary knew God and because she knew Him, she knew she could pray to Him and He would hear her.

SONG OF PRAISE

YOU WILL NEED:
- ☐ Study Journals (1 per girl)
- ☐ Paper (1 per group)
- ☐ Pens (1 per group)

Say: Mary's prayer is special because she was communicating with God and praising Him. God thinks your prayers are special, too. You don't have to pray just like Mary. You can simply share what is on your heart with God. It is pretty incredible to think that we can communicate with the Creator of everything. We can pray bravely and boldly, not because of who we are, but who He is!

Form small groups. Challenge groups to write prayers of praise like Mary's prayer. They can use familiar melodies or make up their own. Lead each group to find and color the names of God in their journals for inspiration (p. 57).

Allow time for each group to practice their song together and then take turns sharing it with the group. If time allows, make a song to a simple melody for the entire group to know and sing together. This song would be a great way to close in prayer.

Small Group Activities

Prayer Bracelets

YOU WILL NEED:

- ☐ Metal washers (available at most hardware stores) (1 per girl)
- ☐ Nail polish (several colors)
- ☐ Colored permanent markers
- ☐ Silk cording or other bracelet string
- ☐ Scissors
- ☐ Decorative bracelet beads

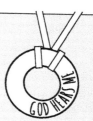

TEACHING TIP:

- ☐ Washers should be 1 1/2" in size or larger for girls to write on the washer with their markers.

Guide the girls to make personalized bracelets that will help them remember God loves to talk and listen to them.

Distribute a metal washer to each girl and guide her to choose a nail polish color to paint the front of her washer. She may have to apply a few coats of polish to the washer. While the washer is drying, guide the girls to measure their wrists with the silk cord provided. Cut a piece of cord the size of each girl's wrist.

Once the washers are dry, lead the girls to string the cord through the back of the washers and tie a knot to secure them in place. Then, they can write or draw something that will encourage them to talk to God (e.g., I am loved, God hears me, praying hands, and so forth).

Next, they can start stringing beads to create their own personal pattern. Once the girls are finished with their bracelets, guide them to secure each end with a knot and tie the ends together.

Say: When we pray we can praise God, ask Him for help, and confess sin to Him. God wants us to pray to Him, confident that He hears and answers our prayers.

Prayer Journal

> **YOU WILL NEED:**
> ☐ Item 10: Prayer Journal (1 per girl, see details on page 65)
> ☐ Construction paper (optional)
> ☐ Staplers
> ☐ Pens
> ☐ Markers

Print a prayer journal for each girl. See page 65 for detailed printing instructions. Guide the girls in assembling their journals by folding the pages and stapling the middle to create a book. Allow them time to decorate their prayer journals.

Complete one day together so that girls will know how to use the prayer journals. Explain each of the sections of the journal and invite the girls to fill it out and practice praying.

Thankful Prayers - Today I am Grateful for...

Say: Thanking God can be very powerful. If you ever struggle with worry, which so many girls do, check out this verse: "Don't worry about anything, but in everything, through prayer and petition with thanksgiving, present your requests to God. And the peace of God, which surpasses all understanding, will guard your hearts and minds in Christ Jesus" (Philippians 4:6-7). Do you see the word *thanksgiving* in this verse? Even when things are hard, we are told by God's true Word to thank Him. It is through prayers of thanksgiving we can experience the peace of God. Write a short thank-you prayer to God.

Confession Prayers - Today I am sorry for this sin...

Say: Sin makes communication with God difficult. First John 1:9 says, "If we confess our sins, he is faithful and righteous to forgive our sins and to cleanse us from all unrighteousness." To confess means to agree with God about our sins. If we want clear communication we need to agree with God about our sin. Write a short "I am sorry" prayer about a specific sin.

Prayer Requests - Today I need God's help with...

Say: God knows what you are going through, but He wants to make sure you talk to Him about it. Sometimes we talk to others about our problems, but we leave God out of that conversation. First John 5:14 tells us, "This is the confidence we have before him: If we ask anything according to his will, he hears us." We can be confident that God hears us, so let's be sure to talk to Him. Share some prayer requests and worries you have with God.

Prayer Praises - Today I see God working in...

Say: Jeremiah 33:3 says, "Call to me and I will answer you and tell you great and incomprehensible things you do not know." God answer prayers. Now remember His ways are not our ways, so the answer may be different than what we asked for, but we can trust Him. So many times we pray prayers and never look back to see how the Lord has answered them. Pause for a minute and write about how you see God working in your life and prayers.

Detailed Printing instructions

Provide for each girl:

- ♡ 1 sheet construction paper (optional)
- ♡ 1 one-sided copy
- ♡ 3+ double-sided copies (select "flip on short edge" option in print settings if applicable)

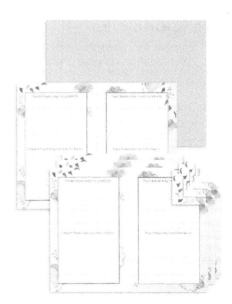

Cut information strip from pages. Stack sheets in the order listed above starting with construction paper on the bottom, or one-sided copy printed side up if not using construction paper.

Staple in center before folding or on edge after folding depending on type of stapler.

Allow girls to decorate their covers with markers or stickers.

Conclusion

YOU WILL NEED:

- ☐ Item 11: CHAT Prayer Stations
- ☐ A large white megaphone
- ☐ Permanent markers
- ☐ Water-soluble paper (1 piece per girl)
- ☐ Bowl of water
- ☐ Blank thank-you notes (1 per girl)
- ☐ Pens (1 per girl)
- ☐ Large newsprint (1 per girl)
- ☐ Markers

TO DO:

- ☐ Print Item 11: CHAT Prayer Stations and cut apart. Place each station's instructions for the girls to read at their designated stations.
- ☐ Set up the prayer stations and allow the girls to work through each station at their own pace. (Station 1: permanent markers, megaphone; Station 2: water-soluble paper, bowl of water; Station 3: blank thank-you notes, pens; Station 4: newsprint, markers)

TEACHING TIP:

- ☐ Prepare the megaphone by writing word descriptions of God on it so the girls know what to do when they arrive at Station 1.

Say: One of the best ways to learn to pray is to start praying. Just like we practice a sport or hobby to grow our muscles and skill, it's important for us to exercise our prayer muscles too!

Lead the girls to notice each prayer station around the room. Explain that each station represents a different way to pray to God using a simple method called CHAT (Cheer, Humble Yourself, Appreciate What God Has Done, and Tell God Your Needs).

Say: I'm going to play some soft music and I want you to take the next several moments to visit each prayer station. As you do, take time to read the instructions at each station and follow the directions. Once everyone has visited all four stations, come back to the center and we will end our time in prayer.

Play soft music and allow the girls time to visit and participate in each station.

Station 1—Cheer
Think about how great our God is. He is so amazing. He deserves our cheers. Take a permanent marker and write on the megaphone some words that describe our great, big God. Then spend some time praying and praising God for being some of the things listed on the megaphone.

Station 2—Humble Yourself
Take a piece of special paper and be honest before God. Write down a sin you need to be sorry for on the paper. Hold the paper in your hand as you pray silently to God saying you are sorry. After you have prayed silently, place your paper in the bowl of water and watch it dissolve away.

Station 3—Appreciation Prayers
When someone does something nice for us, it is kind to take time to write them a thank-you note. How about thanking God for something He has done for you lately? Take a thank-you note and pen and write a note to God specifically thanking Him for something He has done.

Station 4—Tell God Your Needs
Lay down on your newsprint and have a leader or friend trace you. On the outline of your body, take time to write to God different needs, worries, and fears you have. As you write them down, silently pray to God.

After the girls have had time to complete each station, gather the group together and end in prayer.

Pray: *God, thank You for always hearing us and listening to our prayers. God, please help us remember how big You are and how much You love us. Help us believe You are with us even when we feel alone. Thank You for loving us, for providing for us, and for giving us what we need. We love You. In Jesus' name, amen.*

Finish: Girls, I hope you learned something new about God and yourselves today. This week keep exploring who Jesus is and who He made you to be by working through your study journals. Write down any questions or thoughts you may have. Jesus can help you pray fearlessly this week.

Brave to THRIVE WILLINGLY

Leader Bible Study

Have you ever worked really tirelessly at something, only to realize your focus was way off track? Perhaps you thought you were doing what was best or what the Lord wanted only to realize later that your motivations were in the wrong place? If you have ever been in this place in your faith journey, know that you are in good company.

As believers, we should always be growing deeper in our faith, but we may not always do it perfectly. In this last session, the girls you teach will learn more about Martha. Martha often gets a bad reputation for complaining to Jesus that her sister, Mary, didn't help her when Jesus visited their home, but Martha grew in her faith and understanding of what is most important. The next time we see Martha in the Bible she is thriving.

Her brother, Lazarus, had died. When Jesus came to see them it was Mary who stayed at home and Martha who ran to meet Jesus. She was out of the kitchen running hard to the One who could help in their time of need. She was on mission because she was confident in who Jesus is.

Maybe you have gotten a bit distracted in your own walk with the Lord. Often we can lose focus on doing things *for God* instead of spending time *with God*. Be encouraged today that if this resonates with you, you don't have to stay there.

Spend time talking to God today about how you long to sit at His feet and thrive. Praise God for His continued grace and patience as you grow in your faith journey. Then as tomorrow's new mercies rise with the sun, put Him first and soak up time in the presence of God and flourish with a willing heart and spirit.

KEY TRUTH:

God calls me to continue becoming more like Jesus by the power of the Holy Spirit. I can thrive by growing deeper in my faith and living on mission for God.

KEY VERSE:

Yet even now I know that whatever you ask from God, God will give you. John 11:22

KEY PASSAGE:

Martha on a Mission
(Luke 10:38-42; John 11:1-44)

Get Started!

STRETCH AND GROW

YOU WILL NEED:
- [ ] Item 3: Allergy Alert
- [ ] Gummy worms
- [ ] An unopened pack of gummy worms
- [ ] Ruler

TO DO:
- [ ] Print the allergy alert listing the food allergy. Make sure there are enough gummy worms for each girl to use and additional candy to eat.

Give each girl a gummy worm. Explain that the challenge is to see who can stretch her gummy worm the farthest without breaking it. Give each girl time to stretch her worm and measure to see whose worm grew the most. The winner gets a whole, unopened bag of gummy worms.

Allow the girls to eat the remaining gummy worms provided.

Say: Did you know as you follow Jesus you do not stay the same? Just as these worms grew as they were stretched, as you seek Jesus you are stretched and grow to look more like Him. Our goal is not to become longer, like these worms, but to look more and more like Jesus. We can't do that in our own strength, but we can with the help of the Holy Spirit.

Explain: God gave us the Holy Spirit to help us grow. We can thrive (grow, flourish, become stronger) by growing deeper in our faith and living on mission for God. And guess what? You don't have to be perfect to thrive in your relationship with God. You just have to be willing! Pay close attention to today's Bible story as we learn about a woman who grew in her faith to being on mission for Jesus.

Bible Story

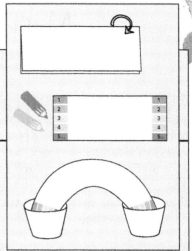

YOU WILL NEED:

☐ Paper towel (See image and instructions below.)
☐ Colored markers
☐ 2 containers of water

TO DO:

☐ Before the session, fold a plain paper towel and color the two ends in the colors of the rainbow (e.g., red, orange, yellow, green, blue, purple, pink). Color each side in the same order of colors.

Say: God created each of us unique and special. We all have different interests, hobbies, talents, and gifts. Our personalities are diverse and unique to exactly who God made us to be. As you continue to grow to look more like Jesus, it is important for you to remember that God made you exactly who you are and He loves you so much. Because He loves you, God doesn't want you to stay the same. He wants you to grow and thrive, to explore and go on adventures and have fun as you enjoy who He made you to be. Let's use this artwork to demonstrate what we are talking about today.

Display the paper towel with colored sides at each end. Place each end of the paper towel in the water and guide the group to watch as the colors spread and make a rainbow.

Say: Isn't that cool? Just like this paper towel soaked up the water and became a beautiful rainbow, God wants us to soak in His truth about who we are. As we believe what God says is true of us, we grow into the beautiful person He created us to be, full of faith, boldness, and bravery as we look to Him.

Continue: Today's Bible story is about a woman who grew in her understanding and faith of who God is. When Jesus came to visit her one day, she had big plans for what she was going to do, but God had even bigger plans to help her grow and learn what it looked like to look to Jesus first. Let's take a look at today's Bible story and find out what happened.

Martha on a Mission
(LUKE 10:38-42, JOHN 11:1-44)

While Jesus and His disciples were traveling, Jesus entered a village, and a woman named Martha welcomed Him into her home. She had a sister named Mary, who sat at the Lord's feet and was listening to what He said. But Martha was distracted by her many tasks, and she came up and asked, "Lord, don't you care that my sister has left me to serve alone? So tell her to give me a hand." The Lord answered her, "Martha, Martha, you are worried and upset about many things, but one thing is necessary. Mary has made the right choice, and it will not be taken away from her."

Some time after this, Mary and Martha's brother, Lazarus, had died. Jesus came to Mary and Martha's home. At this time Lazarus had been in the tomb for four days. Many of the Jews had come to Martha and Mary to comfort them about their brother's death. As soon as Martha heard that Jesus was coming, she went to meet him, but Mary remained seated in the house.

Martha said to Jesus, "Lord, if you had been here, my brother wouldn't have died. Yet even now I know that whatever you ask from God, He will give you."

"Your brother will rise again," Jesus told her.

Martha said to Him, "I know that he will rise again in the resurrection."

Jesus said to her, "I am the resurrection and the life. The one who believes in me, even if he dies, will live. Everyone who lives and believes in me will never die. Do you believe this?"

"Yes, Lord," she told Him, "I believe you are the Messiah, the Son of God, who comes into the world."

Jesus went and mourned His dear friend Lazarus' death and then raised him from the dead. Lazarus came out bound hand and foot with linen strips and with his face wrapped in a cloth. Jesus said to them, "Unwrap him and let him go."

MAKE THE POINT

Say: We are faced with many different choices. Sometimes one choice is better than the other, and other times the choices are simply different. Mary and Martha made two different choices. Martha did not make a bad choice by wanting to serve Jesus, but she missed the best choice—to sit and learn from Jesus. Later, when Martha and Mary's brother, Lazarus, had died, Martha ran to Jesus and met Him. Martha said that she believed Jesus was the Messiah. Even in her grieving of her brother's death, she believed Jesus was the one true God and looked to Him.

Explain: The way Martha responded at the beginning of the story and then again at the end shows how she had grown in her faith and belief of who Jesus was and what was most important. Martha wasn't finished growing in her faith, but the more her faith grew stronger, the more her thoughts, motivations, and actions changed to honor God. **As we continue to grow in our faith, God calls us to continue becoming more like Jesus by the power of the Holy Spirit. We can thrive by growing deeper in our faith and living on mission for God.**

Bible Study

FRUIT PLEASE

> **YOU WILL NEED:**
> ☐ Study Journals (1 per girl)
> ☐ Bibles (1 per girl)
> ☐ Pens (1 per girl)

Say: God calls you to continue becoming more like Jesus. But what does that really look like? Does it mean you carry a bigger Bible or use fancy church words? Let's look at some Scriptures that help us understand what it looks like to thrive with a willing heart in Christ.

Invite the girls to open their journals to "Fruit Please" (pg. 68). Then encourage the girls to open their Bibles to John 15:1-4 and fill in the blanks in that verse.

Say: God calls you to continue becoming more like Jesus by the power of the

Holy Spirit. See, the truth is you can't do it on your own. Apart from Christ we are sinners in need of a Savior.

Ask: What does this passage tell us we need in order to bear fruit? *(Allow the girls to answer, but direct them to the verses for the source of their answers.)*

Say: These verses tell us we need to remain connected to God to bear fruit. We cannot do it by ourselves. As believers, we are connected to God by the Holy Spirit living inside of us. Without that, we can't thrive and bear fruit.

Instruct the girls to open their Bibles to Galatians 5:22-23. On the fruit on their journal page, encourage them to list a different fruit of the Spirit on each piece of fruit.

Say: Many times we think being kind, having joy, showing patience, or being faithful is a result of working harder, but that is not the case. We can't just wake up and decide to be gentle all on our own anymore than we can decide to wake up and be an apple tree. Love, joy, peace, patience, kindness, goodness, faithfulness, gentleness, and self-control are the result of a life rooted in Christ and thriving by the power of the Holy Spirit.

Thriving or Not Thriving

YOU WILL NEED:
- ☐ Study Journals (1 per girl)
- ☐ Pens (1 per girl)

Invite the girls to open their journals to "Thriving or Not Thriving" (pg. 69). Explain that there are review statements about Martha from today's Bible story. From each statement, the girls will decide on their own if Martha was thriving or not thriving by her actions. Remind the girls that to thrive means to grow, flourish, or advance in their relationship with God. If they believe Martha was thriving, they will color in the flower beside the question. If they do not believe she was thriving, they will color in the empty pot. Allow the girls time to mark their answers in their journals.

Say: When Jesus came to visit, Martha was distracted by her many tasks. *(Allow the girls to share what they chose as an answer.)*

Ask: Why did you choose your answer?

Say: Martha was not thriving at this point. Jesus had come into her home, but Scripture says she was distracted by her many tasks. Now before we start judging Martha, we too can get distracted and miss time with Jesus.

Ask: What are some things that distract you? (*Allow the girls to respond.*)

Say: Martha complained to Jesus and told Him to ask Mary to help her.

Ask: Why did you choose your answer? (*Allow the girls to respond.*)

Say: Again, Jesus is in Martha's home and instead of being with Him, she is tattling on her sister. She wasn't thriving because she wasn't concerned with the most important thing that was literally right in front of her.

Say: After her brother died, Martha heard Jesus was on His way and instead of waiting for Him to arrive, she ran out to meet Him.

Ask: Thriving or nor thriving, what did you choose? (*Allow the girls to respond.*)

Say: Sometimes Martha is judged as the *bad* sister because she was distracted when Jesus came to her house, but Martha learned and grew from that lesson. After her brother died, she didn't just wait for Jesus. She ran to meet Him because she knew He could help. This time she was thriving.

Ask: When you are going through a hard time, do you sit back and worry, or do you run to spend time in prayer with Jesus because He can meet your needs? (*Allow the girls to respond.*)

Say: When Martha came to Jesus, even though her brother had been dead for four days she said to Him, "Yet even now I know that whatever you ask from God, God will give you" (John 11:22).

Ask: Which did you choose: thriving or not thriving? (*Allow the girls to respond.*)

Say: This girl is seriously thriving. She is growing bold and is confident not in who she is but in who God is.

Ask: Now when it comes to you, do you consider yourself to be thriving or not thriving and why? (*Allow the girls to reflect and respond if they feel comfortable.*)

Say: Throughout our study together we have looked at what the Bible teaches us about God and how that leads us to live bravely for Him. As a believer, you know you are called to be different from those around you who don't know Jesus. You know bravery means to trust in Jesus daily and follow Him, but you also experience the everyday struggle to live bravely knowing your identity and purpose depend on the truth of who God is, not what you do.

Continue: As we continue to grow in our faith and take bold steps to obey and follow Jesus, it is important to check our hearts and motivations to make sure we are thriving and growing willingly—because our hearts have been changed by Jesus, not because we are trying to earn God's attention. We are all at different places in our spiritual journey, and that is OK! Wherever we are, God wants us to continue on—learning more about Him, recognizing where our source of truth, courage, love, and growth comes from, and growing to look more and more like Jesus in our actions, words, and attitudes. **As we continue to grow in our faith, God calls us to continue becoming more like Jesus by the power of the Holy Spirit. We can thrive by growing deeper in our faith and living on mission for God.**

Small Group Activities

On Mission

> **YOU WILL NEED:**
> ☐ Pack of playing cards (1 per group)

Invite the girls to form smaller groups. Explain that their challenge is to see who can build the tallest card tower in the allotted amount of time. Give each group their cards and call *begin*. As these groups work hard to build their towers, ask adult leaders to play a different role. Adults will subtly try to hinder their progress by talking to the girls, distracting them, slipping some of their cards away, or even giving unhelpful instructions. After adults try to distract the girls' efforts, lead them to help build the tower and give back the cards taken.

While the groups may grow frustrated, be sure to encourage them not to give up on their mission to build the tallest card tower. After they have struggled but had some success, judge the tallest tower and then circle up for some discussion.

Ask:

♥ How did you feel during this mission?

♥ What made it easy or difficult?

♥ Did you ever feel like giving up? Why or why not?

Say: Being on mission is tough work. Girls, when you are living for Jesus there will be tough times. There will be times you want to give up. There will be people who don't understand or who will try to discourage you from following God's plan. You can give up or you can bravely thrive as you live on mission for God. Here's the great reminder: Martha wasn't perfect. She missed sitting at Jesus' feet because she was too busy in the kitchen serving. She could have given up and labeled herself as a failure, but she chose to continue to seek Jesus. Remember, you don't live on mission alone. God calls you to continue becoming more like Jesus by the power of the Holy Spirit. You can thrive by growing deeper in your faith and living on mission for God.

Holy Spirit Helper

YOU WILL NEED:

☐ Several gallon size bags with random items like: interlocking blocks, some coins, small office supplies, small toys, and so forth
☐ Pencils and paper (1 per group)

Prepare the bags with the selected items. It is best to have more items so that it is difficult for the group to remember everything that is in the bags. Place the bags on a table and cover them with a blanket. Explain to the group that during this next activity the goal is to remember as many items as possible that were in the bag. You will uncover the bag and everyone has one minute to look at the bag and try to remember everything in it. One person, the scribe, is given a paper and pencil so that they can quickly record everything they see.

After a minute, cover up the bag and give the girls time to try and list everything they saw in the bag on a separate sheet of paper. When they need help they can ask the scribe to remind them of things they had written down in hopes of getting all the items listed. Play several rounds with different bags and different scribes. Then circle up and discuss this activity.

Ask:

♡ Was it easy or difficult to remember all the items in each bag? Why or why not?

♡ How was the scribe helpful?

♡ Is it easy or hard to remember everything we learn about God? Why?

♡ How is the Holy Spirit like the scribe for us?

Say: Living on mission for God can get difficult and we need help remembering things. Just like the scribe in this game helped you remember things you may have forgotten, the Holy Spirit helps you remember the things of God. He is our Helper. Through His power we can grow to live more like Jesus and be on mission for God. He helps us bravely thrive with a willing heart.

Continue: Remember, thrive means to grow and mature. After we receive Jesus as Savior, God doesn't want to leave us where we are. He longs for us to grow in our faith and look more like Jesus. Through the power of the Holy Spirit you can be brave and thrive.

Conclusion

YOU WILL NEED:

☐ Foam cups (1 per girl)
☐ Potting soil
☐ Seeds
☐ Water
☐ Markers

Give each girl a foam cup and a marker. Explain that today they will plant their own plants. The goal of a plant is to see it grow, change, and thrive.

Say: For a plant to grow and thrive it needs help, right? What does a plant need? *(Allow the girls to answer things like, sun, water, soil, and so forth.)* Okay, let's write those things around our cups. Let's write *good soil*, *water*, and *sunlight* on the sides of our cups. *(Allow time for the girls to write these items.)*

Continue: Now for you to live on mission for God and to thrive, what are some things you need? Before you answer, let's compare them to the three we listed above. Let's look at your soil. For you to grow and live bravely for Jesus, you need good soil—a strong foundation of what you believe. Your faith in Jesus and what you believe about God need to be strong. Next to the word *soil* on your cup, write the words *foundation of faith*. Next you all mentioned water. Just as a plant needs water to grow, we need to make sure we are drinking from the well of living water that is God's Word. If the time you spent in God's Word was how much water your plant got, what shape do you think it might be in? Next to the word *water* on your cup, write *God's Word*. Lastly, just as the plant needs time in the sunshine to grow, we need to spend time with the Son of God in prayer. Communicating with God helps us be brave as we live on mission for Him. Next to the word *sun* on your cup, write *prayer*.

After the cups have been decorated, instruct the girls to add soil, seeds, and water to their cups. Challenge them to place their plants somewhere in their homes where they will get sun and they will remember to water them. As they see their cups, encourage them to remember that they can thrive by willingly pursuing Jesus and growing deeper in their faith.

Finish: Girls, I am so glad that we have been able to learn more about God and ourselves through this study. As we keep learning more about Him and how much He loves us, always remember that you are God's brave girl and He has called you to be brave. You can courageously and fearlessly live with bold faith, not in your own strength but because of who He made you to be.

See Your Family's Faith Bloom

Great Resources for Tween Girls and Their Parents

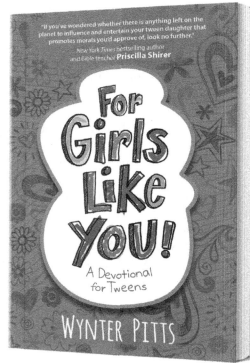

This daily devotional from Wynter Pitts opens girls' eyes to the truth about who God made them to be and the difference it makes in their lives. Each devotion includes a special prayer girls can share with God.

◀ Wynter and her husband, Jonathan, parents of four girls, give practical advice and encouragement to equip you in your parenting journey and to help improve your daughter's relationship with God, with you, and with the world around her.

HARVEST HOUSE

Discover these and more family faith-building resources at Lifeway.com